CW00375530

Workbook 13

Building a High Performance Team

Manage People
Certificate
S/NVQ Level 4

Institute of Management Open Learning Programme

Series editor: Gareth Lewis
Author: Lisa Davis

chartered
management
institute

Pergamon
Flexible
Learning

OXFORD AMSTERDAM BOSTON LONDON NEW YORK PARIS
SAN DIEGO SANFRANCISCO SINGAPORE SYDNEY TOKYO

Pergamon Flexible Learning
An imprint of Elsevier Science
Linacre House, Jordan Hill, Oxford OX2 8DP
200 Wheeler Road, Burdington, MA 01803
A division of Reed Educational and Professional Publishing Ltd

First published 1997
Reprinted 1999, 2000, 2002, 2003

© Institute of Management Foundation 1997

All rights reserved. No part of this publication may be reproduced in
any material form (including photocopying or storing in any medium by
electronic means and whether or not transiently or incidentally to some
other use of this publication) without the written permission of the
copyright holder except in accordance with the provisions of the Copyright,
Designs and Patents Act 1988 or under the terms of a licence issued by the
Copyright Licensing Agency Ltd, 90 Tottenham Court Road, London,
England W1T ALP. Applications for the copyright holder's written
permission to reproduce any part of this publication should be addressed
to the publishers

British Library Cataloguing in Publication Data
A catalogue record for this book is available from the British Library

ISBN 0 7506 3671 8

For more information on all Pergamon Flexible Learning
publications please visit our website at www.Pergamonfl.com

Typeset by Avocet Typeset, Brill, Aylesbury, Bucks
Printed and bound in Great Britain

Contents

Series overview

The Institute of Management Open Learning Programme is a series of workbooks prepared by the Institute of Management and Pergamon Open Learning for managers seeking to develop themselves.

Comprising seventeen open learning workbooks, the programme covers the best of modern management theory and practice, and each workbook provides a range of frameworks and techniques to improve your effectiveness as a manager, thus helping you acquire the knowledge and skill to make you fully competent in your role.

Each workbook is written by an experienced management writer and covers an important management topic or theme. The activities both reinforce learning and help to relate the generic ideas to your individual work context. While coverage of each topic is fully comprehensive, additional reading suggestions and reference sources are given for those who wish to study to a greater depth.

Designed to be practical, stimulating and challenging, the aim of the workbooks is to improve performance at work by benefiting you and your organization. This practical focus is at the heart of the competence based approach that has been adopted by the programme.

The structure of the programme

The design and overall structure of the programme has two main organizing principles, both of which are closely linked to the national standards for management developed by the MCI (Management Charter Initiative).

First, the workbooks are grouped according to the key roles of management.

- Underpinning the management standards are a series of **personal competences** which describe the personal skills required by all managers, which are essential to skill in all the main functional or key role areas.
- **Manage Activities** describes the principles of managing processes and activities, with service to the customer as an essential part of this.
- **Manage Resources** describes the acquisition, control and monitoring of financial and other resources.
- **Manage People** looks at the key skills involved in leadership, developing one's staff and managing their performance.

■ **Manage Information** discusses the acquisition, storage and use of information for communication, problem solving and decision making.

In addition, there are three specialized key roles: **Manage Quality, Manage Projects** and **Manage Energy**. The workbooks cover the first two of these. Unlike the four primary key roles above, these are not compulsory for certificate, diploma or S/NVQ requirements, but provide options for the latter.

Together, these key roles provide a comprehensive description of the fundamental principles of management as it applies in any organization – commercial, maintained sector or not-for-profit.

Second, the programme is organized according to **levels of management**, seniority and responsibility.

Level 4 represents first line management. In accredited programmes this is equivalent to S/NVQ Level 4, Certificate in Management or CMS. Level 5 is equivalent to middle/senior management and is accredited at S/NVQ Level 5, Diploma in Management or DMS. There are two S/NVQs at Level 5: Operational Management and Strategic Management. The operations role is focussed internally within an organization on the maintenance of systems and standards of output, whilst the strategic role is focussed on the whole organization, including the external operating environment, and looks at setting directions.

Together, the workbooks cover all the background knowledge you need to have for all units of competence in the MCI standards at Level 4 and Level 5 (apart from the specialized units in the key role Manage Energy). They also provide skills development and opportunities for portfolio building.

For a comprehensive list of workbooks, see page ix. For a comprehensive list of links with the standards, see the *User Guide*.

How to use the programme

The programme is deliberately designed to be flexible and can be used in a variety of ways:

■ to update on important management topics and themes, or develop individual skills: as the workbooks are grouped according to themes, it should be easy for you to pick out one that suits your needs

■ as part of generic management development programmes: you can choose the modules that fit the themes of the programme

- as part of, and in support of, accredited competence-based programmes.

For N/SVQs at both Levels 4 and 5, there are options in the combinations of units that make up the various awards. By using the map provided in the *User Guide*, individuals will be able to select the workbooks appropriate to their specific needs, and their chosen accreditation options. Some of the activities will help you provide evidence for your portfolio; where we think this is the case, we give the relevant reference to the standards.

For Certificate or CMS, Diploma or DMS, individuals should choose modules that not only meet their individual needs but also satisfy the requirements of the delivering body and the awarding body.

You may need help and guidance in these choices, and the *User Guide* sets out the options and advice in much more detail. A fuller description of the potential uses of this material in evidence gathering and portfolio building can also be found in the *User Guide*, as can a detailed description of the contents of each workbook.

Workbooks in the Institute of Management Open Learning Programme

Personal Competences (Levels 4 and 5)

  1 *The Influential Manager**
  2 *Managing Yourself**

Manage Activities (Level 4)

  3 *Understanding Business Process Management*
  4 *Customer Focus*

Manage Activities (Level 5)

  5 *Getting TQM to Work*
  6 *Leading from the Front*
  7 *Improving Your Organization's Success*

Manage Resources (Level 4)

  8 *Project Management*
  9 *Budgeting and Financial Control*

Manage Resources (Level 5)

  10 *Effective Financial and Resource Management*

Manage People (Level 4)

  1 *The Influential Manager*
  2 *Managing Yourself*
  11 *Getting the Right People to do the Right Job*
  12 *Developing Yourself and Your Staff*
  13 *Building a High Performance Team*

An asterisk indicates that a particular workbook also contains material suitable for a particular key role or personal competence.

Links to qualifications

S/NVQ programmes

This workbook can help candidates to achieve credit and develop skills in the key role Manage People at Level 4, and covers the following units and elements:

C13   Manage the performance of teams and individuals
C13.1   Allocate work to teams and individuals
C13.2   Agree objectives and work plans with teams and individuals
C13.3   Assess the performance of teams and individuals
C13.4   Provide feedback on their performance to teams and individuals

The unit C13 is also an option in Level 5 Operational Management.

Certificate and Diploma programmes

This workbook, together with two core workbooks (1 – *The Influential Manager* and 2 – *Manage Yourself*) and the two other Level 4 workbooks on managing people (11 – *Getting the Right People to do the Right Job* and 12 – *Developing Yourself and Your Staff*), covers all of the knowledge required in the key role Manage People for Certificate in Management and CMS programmes.

Links to qualifications

The other workbook in the key role Manage People at Level 4 are:

1 *The Influential Manager*
2 *Managing Yourself*
11 *Getting the Right People to do the Right Job*
12 *Developing Yourself and Your Staff*

and at Level 5:

14 *The New Model Leader*

Introduction

Team building is a key managerial skill. Building a high performance team is often the most difficult and demanding task a manager is required to undertake. People, unlike systems, processes and procedures, are highly individual, extremely unpredictable and frequently troublesome. Blending a group of distinct personalities into a team is not easy. It is, though, extremely rewarding, and well worth the effort.

Managers who never quite acquire the trick of team building often find themselves stumbling from drama to crisis, hoping that things will get better and longing for retirement. Managers who can build a team, using a judicious combination of team role recognition, motivation and performance management, find that life – although not perfect – is much easier and more satisfying.

In this workbook we will be focusing on the key skills of recognizing and understanding team roles, using motivation and carrying out performance management reviews.

Objectives

By the end of this Workbook you should be able to:

- Identify the key factors which must be present within a high performance team
- Recognize your own preferred team role, and the preferred team role of each person in your team
- Allocate work tasks in accordance with each team member's preferences and strengths
- Put motivation theory into practice to encourage people to work willingly and well
- Identify job key result areas and the appropriate objectives for each area
- Undertake regular performance reviews
- Provide appropriate feedback to your people

Section I What is a high performance team?

What is a high performance team?

A high performance team is much more than a group of people who happen to work for the same company. A high performance team is a team which:

- works together as a cohesive unit
- is keen to perform well
- takes pride in the team

In this first section of the Workbook we shall be looking at the key characteristics and key elements of a high performance team.

The difference between a group and a team

If you want to build a high performance team, then you need to begin by understanding the key differences between a group of people who happen to work together, and a team of people who hold the same vision for success.

ACTIVITY 1

Consider the differences between a group of people who happen to work together and a high performance team, and then complete the chart below.

Key characteristics of a group of people who happen to work together	Key characteristics of a high performance team
1 2 3	1 2 3

FEEDBACK

Some examples of high performance teams are:

■   orchestras, television, theatre, opera and dance company teams

■   radio, television and newspaper journalist teams

■   hospital, fire brigade, paramedic and police teams

Each of these teams are closely aligned towards achieving a very specific objective such as, for example:

■   broadcast the news at 9 p.m.

■   publish a 32-page newspaper every day, Monday to Friday

■   perform *Madam Butterfly* to a live audience every night for a week

■   remove an appendix

■   deliver a baby

■   resuscitate an unconscious patient

■   put out a fire

■   track down a serial killer

Alignment to a common goal alone is not sufficient to produce high performance. Teams which consistently produce results and which work well together also exhibit a number of additional qualities.

Key characteristics of a group of people who happen to work together	Key characteristics of a high performing team
People	*People*
1 Work independently, often to their own agenda, invariably putting their own needs first	1 Work co-operatively, invariably putting the needs of the team and the team's objective at the top of their priority list
2 Are reluctant to accept additional responsibility on the basis that they: ■ are not prepared to carry the can if things go wrong ■ are not paid to undertake additional or complex tasks ■ are not willing to sacrifice the time or the energy	2 Are prepared to do whatever it takes to achieve the team's objective. In practice, this may mean that responsibility is shared equally, or that some people take on extra tasks and have to go the extra mile, for the good of the team
3 Have difficulty trusting other team members and feel that they have to: ■ watch their backs ■ be careful about what they say ■ avoid disclosing any information which could be used against them, either personally or professionally ■ avoid admitting any mistakes or errors of judgement	3 Make a real effort to build strong relationships with other team members, and consciously work towards a climate where they are able to: ■ communicate openly and honestly; e.g. discuss feelings, ideas, opinions, problems, successes ■ ask team members for support, feedback, advice and guidance ■ admit mistakes and share concerns ■ respect the individual contribution which team member makes to the team
4 Step out of the team when serious problems occur, saying things like: ■ I never thought it would work ! ■ It was bad planning, right from the start ... ■ I'm going to put this behind me and get on with the important stuff ...	4 Forge even stronger links when problems occur, saying things like: ■ 'We've done it before, we can do it again!' ■ 'How can we make this work?' ■ 'There has to be a way ... and we'll find it'
5 Are critical of the group leader, but are unwilling to make decisions or take the initiative without the leader's direction and supervision	5 Support the team leader wholeheartedly, and are prepared to take decisions or act in the leader's absence
6 Are unable to deal with disagreements in a constructive way. Jealousy, impatience, intolerance, gossip, rumour-mongering and back-biting are fairly usual	6 When team members disagree, there is an open and honest exchange of views and opinions. People actively seek a win/win outcome or say: 'Privately – within the team – I may disagree with you, but I'll support you in public' or 'OK – let's agree to disagree ... and get on with the job'
7 Are unwilling to take any responsibility for the progress or development of the group	7 Are prepared to take responsibility for the well-being, progress and development of the team
8 Do not feel that they owe any loyalty to the group or the individual people within the group	8 Express loyalty to the team through words and actions – because the team is important to them

So, the key attributes of high performing teams are:

■ alignment to a common objective
■ co-operation

- motivation
- communication
- positive response to external pressures

The next activity will give you an opportunity to assess some of the teams in which you have participated as a team member.

ACTIVITY 2

Identify three teams in which you have participated as a team member or a team leader:

- team 1 should be the **best** team in which you have ever been involved
- team 2 should be the **worst** team in which you have ever been involved
- team 3 should be a team in which you are **currently** involved

Now complete the chart below by allocating points to each team for each key attribute.

5 = excellent   4 = good   3 = reasonable   2 = patchy

1 = poor   0 = diabolical

For example:

	Alignment	Co-operation	Motivation	Communication	Response to pressure
Best team	5 4 ● 3 2 1 0	5 ● 4 3 2 1 0	5 4 3 ● 2 1 0	5 4 ● 3 2 1 0	5 ● 4 3 2 1 0

	Alignment	Co-operation	Motivation	Communication	Response to pressure
Best team	5 4 3 2 1 0	5 4 3 2 1 0	5 4 3 2 1 0	5 4 3 2 1 0	5 4 3 2 1 0

	Alignment	Co-operation	Motivation	Communication	Response to pressure
Worst team	5 4 3 2 1 0	5 4 3 2 1 0	5 4 3 2 1 0	5 4 3 2 1 0	5 4 3 2 1 0

	Alignment	Co-operation	Motivation	Communication	Response to pressure
Current team	5	5	5	5	5
	4	4	4	4	4
	3	3	3	3	3
	2	2	2	2	2
	1	1	1	1	1
	0	0	0	0	0

FEEDBACK

Your answers to this activity will, of course, be strictly personal to you and will reflect **your perceptions** of **your teams**. No matter how you responded, it is fair to say that the teams which perform well together and consistently achieve and exceed their targets are those which are high-scoring in the key attribute areas.

Hopefully, your current team will have achieved a high-scoring profile. If not, by the time you have completed this Workbook, you will have the tools and techniques which will enable you, at the very least, to contribute towards improved alignment, co-operation, motivation, communication and positive response to pressure.

Team alignment

Team alignment is about sharing a vision, a goal and a strategy. For example:

- **shared vision**   To make and sell the best tasting pizzas in the UK
- **shared goal**   To take 75% of market share by December 1997
- **shared strategy**   To use the highest quality ingredients to make a product which meets our specification irrespective of external forces

Problems occur when:

- right from the start, not everyone on the team understands or shares the same vision, goal or strategy
  or
- the team starts off sharing these concepts, but later, when external pressures are exerted, the team divides into opposing factions

For example:

January 1996: launch of project

■ **shared vision**   To make and sell the best tasting pizzas in the UK
percentage of team: 100 per cent

■ **shared goal**   To take 75 per cent of market share by December
1997
percentage of team: 100 per cent

■ **shared strategy**   To use the highest quality ingredients to make a
product which meets our specification
percentage of team: 100 per cent

January 1997: mid-way through project

■ **shared vision**   To make and sell the best tasting pizzas in the UK
percentage of team: 30 per cent
To make and sell a pizza which compares in taste to
the current brand leader
percentage of team: 70 per cent

■ **shared goal**   To take 75 per cent of market share by December
1997
percentage of team: 100 per cent

■ **shared strategy**   To use the highest quality ingredients to make a
product which meets our specification
percentage of team: 30 per cent
To use good quality ingredients in order to make a
product which is competitively priced
percentage of team: 70 per cent

The next activity will give you an opportunity to check the extent of your
current team's alignment.

ACTIVITY 3

1 Begin by completing the chart below. (Use a separate piece of paper if you wish to preserve confidentiality.)
2 When you have identified, on paper, your perception of the team's vision, goal and strategy, check how these key elements are perceived by at least three other members of your team.
3 Compare your responses with their responses. Is there total alignment?

Part 1 For you to complete:

My team's shared vision is:
My team's shared goal is:
My team's shared strategy is:

Part 2

Ask three members of your team to complete the boxes below (answers can be supplied on separate sheets of paper to preserve confidentiality, if required).

Team member 1
My team's shared vision is:
My team's shared goal is:
My team's shared strategy is:

Team member 2
My team's shared vision is:
My team's shared goal is:
My team's shared strategy is:

Team member 3
My team's shared vision is:
My team's shared goal is:
My team's shared strategy is:

Part 3

(a) My perception of the team's shared vision, goal and strategy is identical to my colleagues' perception of these factors. We are completely aligned.

yes ☐   no ☐

(b) There are some differences between my perceptions and my colleagues' perceptions of these factors.

yes ☐   no ☐

(c) There are so many differences in perception that I wonder if we are all members of the same team.

yes ☐   no ☐

If you are completely aligned with your colleagues, then there is probably nothing further you need to do in this direction. If, however:

■ there are differences in the way in which these three team members perceive vision, goal and strategy

■ you suspect that there are other people on the team who have different perceptions then it's time to take action.

IMPROVING TEAM ALIGNMENT

A good way to get everyone singing from the same song-sheet is to call a high-priority team meeting.

■ arrange the meeting at a time when everyone is able to attend. (No excuses for non-attendance are acceptable. Let people know you really mean business)

■ at the meeting ask the team to brainstorm:

- the team's vision
- the team's objective
- the team's strategy

    Note: your role at this stage is to write down the contributions generated by the brainstorming process.

    Remember:

- All contributions are equally valid and important
- Every contribution is acceptable, no matter how irrelevant, imaginative, inappropriate or off-the-wall
- Write down every contribution **exactly** as it is given to you
- Write on flipchart paper (A1 size) using thick blue or black markers, so that everyone in the room can see what has been written
- Don't attempt to paraphrase or improve the contributions
- Don't **comment** on or **criticize** the contributions, and don't react, even if you think something is patently stupid or erroneous
- When everyone has exhausted all possibilities and the list is complete, pin or Blu-Tak the sheets around the room

- pin up your own flip chart sheet which lists **your** perceptions of the team's vision, goal and strategy
- Enthusiastically describe and explain your vision, goal and strategy. Make it exciting. Make people want to be part of it by explaining how the organization, the team and everyone on the team will benefit. (Everyone wants to be successful. Everyone, deep down, would like to contribute and be part of a winning, high-performing team)
- Highlight the similarities between your perceptions and individual team members' perceptions. Whatever you do – even if it applies – don't throw your hands up in horror and say 'Is it any wonder we're not achieving … we're all trying to do different things!' The team will quickly see that for themselves. Your task here is to bring people closer together, not drive them further apart
- Explain the concept of alignment and why it's so important for high performance teams
- Bring the team into alignment by asking:

    'If we are to achieve this vision, this goal, this strategy,
    what do we need to do in the next 6 months?'

- Ask the team to either brainstorm again, or work in pairs to generate a list of ideas. These should be practical steps which the team can put into action – e.g.:
    - 'Let's schedule an extra weekly team meeting every Monday morning so that we can meet for breakfast to prepare an action plan for the week'
    - 'Let's create a new system to obtain feedback from customers'.
- Ask the team to feed back all the suggestions they have generated and, again, list them on a flipchart so everyone can see
- Invite the team to prioritize the suggestions. You can do this by asking each team member to vote for their preferred top three suggestions
- Set an agreed target date for implementation of the top three suggestions

Team co-operation

Individual members of high performance teams co-operate with one another – even when it means that the co-operation may involve some level of personal inconvenience, e.g:

■ 'OK – you can have the notes I prepared'
  (even though it took me three weeks to get them ready and I was hoping I would be able to go to the meeting myself)

■ 'Yes, I'll stay overnight in Scotland on Tuesday and go and see Harry for you on Wednesday'
  (even though I can't stand Harry and I would prefer not to stay over)

Team co-operation doesn't happen overnight: 'OK, we're a team – we'll co-operate!' Team co-operation exists when:

■ team members feel that the workload is shared equally among everyone. Tasks are allocated fairly and in accordance with each person's strengths. Everyone understands that the team, as a whole, will only achieve its objectives if each individual completes the tasks which have been lined up for him or her

■ everyone on the team feels equal in every respect. Information is shared equally and at the same time, so that everyone knows what is going on

■ everyone has the same right to contribute ideas, present their views and disagree with the others on the team. No-one is ever excluded because they hold a different view from the mainstream

■ everyone is treated in the same way. There are no favourites or black sheep. There are no cliques or specially favoured groups

■ people feel confident that if they need help or support from the team – no matter what – it will be forthcoming

Team motivation

Motivation is the driving force that makes us do things – even the things that we would prefer not to have to do. Although we'll be looking at motivation in detail in the next section of this Workbook, the key point to remember is that we:

■ **do things** in order to **receive** and **enjoy the pleasure** of a reward of some kind. For example, we go out for dinner in order to enjoy the pleasure of eating good food and, maybe, drinking fine wine. We spend time with people we like so that we can enjoy the pleasure of their company.

■ **avoid doing things** in order to **avoid** the **pain** which is likely to arise out of the activity. For example, we avoid ending a relationship because we don't want to experience the pain of feeling guilty. We avoid ringing the bank manager because we don't want to hear bad news.

You can increase team motivation by increasing the amount of rewards your team members enjoy as a result of being part of the team. As we will see further on in this Workbook, these prizes need have nothing to do with money or material rewards – they can be connected to prestige, recognition, security, self-esteem and so on.

Team communication

Effective team communication is about:

- individuals on the team being able to share ideas and express opinions honestly, openly, without competitiveness or fear of failure
- the team, as a unit, communicating so that everyone on the team is clear about what is supposed to happen, who is doing what, and whether or not the team, as a unit, is achieving its objectives
- the team, and the team leader, communicating with one voice with the rest of the world. In this context, the rest of the world means anyone and everyone who isn't part of the team

Response to pressure

Sometimes teams can appear to be working well but, at the first sign of external pressure, they fall apart. External pressure can take many forms, including:

- External to the organization:
  stiff opposition from competitors
  - 'everything we've done over the past three years has been a waste of time because Jordan's team has beaten us to it. ... so it's back to the drawing board'
  - 'we've lost the race – they're bringing out their version, and it's 20 per cent cheaper than ours'
  - 'this new government legislation means we can't go ahead'
  - 'the DTI won't give us a licence – so the project has been scrapped'
- Internal, within the organization
  - 'Brian's pulled the plug on the budget – there's no more money for us'
  - 'they're closing Cardiff, so it means we can't expand the project'
  - 'they're bringing in some computer PhD to look at what we've done'
  - 'we've got three months to get this right ... or we're out'

Groups and weak teams often collapse under external pressure and it becomes a case of 'everyone for themselves'. In these circumstances, the concept of the team disappears and each individual shifts into *damage limitation* – looking to see how he can best minimize the damage to his own position and his own career. High performance teams often grow stronger when faced with external pressure – 'we've come this far, they're not going to stop us now'. The NASA Space Team is a good example of a high performance team which watched the lives of close colleagues, years of work and billions of dollars go up in smoke and flames. They didn't fall apart. They picked themselves up, dusted themselves off and looked at how they could prevent a similar tragedy from ever happening again.

You can help the team to respond positively to external pressure by:

■ working as hard as you are asking everyone else to work
■ maintaining an air of optimism (even if you feel like shooting yourself)
■ saying what you mean and meaning what you say
■ keeping your temper and keeping your head
■ treating everyone with respect, fairness and good manners

If the key factors for success are to exist – alignment, co-operation, motivation, communication and positive response to external pressure – then it is important to understand the complex process which enables a group of disparate individuals to meld together into a cohesive, and effective, unit.

Forming, Storming, Norming and Performing

Tuckman[1] has identified that teams – a group of people brought together by circumstance to perform a task and produce a result – work through four, quite separate, stages:

1 Forming
2 Storming
3 Norming
4 Performing

FORMING

Here you have a group of people, some of whom may be enthusiastic volunteers, some of whom may be unwilling conscripts. Some people within the group may already know one another, while others will be complete strangers. Some of the group may be drawn together because they share certain factors in common – perhaps they work for the same function, or enjoy the same pay-scale, or live in the same geographical area, or have attained similar qualifications. Other members of the group may have quite different backgrounds, values, interests, beliefs, career aspirations. In most instances, at the start of the forming stage, the group (a) have not yet bought into the group's objective and (b) almost every member of the group will have a different personal agenda:

- 'I'm here because I want to make sure that they aren't going to interfere with what Marketing is trying to do ...'
- 'I don't even want to be here – but I'm the only person who can use the software ...'
- 'Mike said he thought I ought to be part of this – it could help me when I apply for the London job ...'
- 'I think it's a fantastic opportunity to do something new ...'

STORMING

At this second stage of the process, group members have been given the team's objective and have each been assigned their own individual task. This is when the problems start:

- 'I don't want to have to research all that information – it's going to take forever ...'
- 'Well, what's Sandra supposed to be doing?'
- 'I don't see why we have to meet every week ...'
- 'I don't think one team meeting a week is enough at this stage ...'
- 'I should be looking after the budget – I'm an accountant!'
- 'the people from Liverpool don't seem to be taking this seriously ...'

NORMING

At the third stage, individual team members start to settle down a bit and begin to work together in a reasonably civilized way. People do their jobs, attend meetings when they are supposed to and make some kind of an effort to rub along together. Team communication is reasonable (although some members find it easier to communicate more openly and honestly with some colleagues rather than with everyone). Team motivation peaks and dips; it is high when things are going smoothly, low when problems occur. The team may hold together for a little while in the face of external pressure, but will eventually fragment and fall apart when the going gets really tough. Sadly, many teams never progress beyond the Norming stage.

PERFORMING

Once people begin to Perform as a team, miraculous and amazing things can begin to occur. You may have observed this when watching some kinds of sport – everyone on the team knows precisely where everyone else is; tricky moves are executed smoothly and speedily; successes are wholeheartedly celebrated; errors are rectified without criticism. In Performing teams everyone gives of their best – not because they **have** to, but because they **want to.**

ACTIVITY 4

Cast your mind back to a team of which you have been a member. Think about the kinds of behaviours – actions and communication – the people in your team displayed at each of these four stages. Complete the chart below.

Stage	Actions and communication
1 Group forming	
2 Group storming	
3 Group norming	
4 Group performing	

FEEDBACK

1 GROUP FORMING

At this first stage, when people first come together as a group, on the surface they will tend to be on their best behaviour. At a deeper, personal level there will be considerable anxiety – will I fit in? will I be accepted? will I be able to do it? will I be able to cope? Those people with something in common will tend to gravitate towards one another and the group may look something like Figure 1 below.

Sub-group 1 The people from Manchester	**Team Leader**	Sub-group 4 Diane and Mark – the two most senior people	
Sub-group 2 Tom and Jane from the lab	Sub-group 3 Melissa – newly appointed		Sub-group 5 Adrian – been with the company for 20 years

Figure 1   Possible arrangement of people within a group at the Forming stage

There will be some jostling for position to achieve a close, meaningful, special relationship with the team leader, as people may feel that this might minimize some of the potential danger they perceive within the situation – 'I'll be all right if I get on the right side of him'.

People with specialist knowledge, information or connections will often trot out everything they know in an attempt to impress the others. Senior people may take a back seat – 'I'm really only here as an observer' – while people with a long service record may take the view: 'I've seen them come, and I've seen them go'.

Everyone will be cautious and contained, watching to see how everyone else is behaving, and making an effort to fit in and not to be too conspicuous. There is very little authenticity or genuine exchange of feelings: 'No, no – you go ahead – I don't mind at all'.

2 GROUP STORMING

This is when life gets really interesting, particularly for the team leader. At this stage of the process conflict arises between individuals and sub-groups. There is resistance to everything – control, the demands of the team's task, the team leader. Everyone thinks their way is best and no one can understand why others can't see that. The only point on which most people agree at this stage is that the team leader 'couldn't lead them out of a paper bag'. When the group is Storming, anarchy rules. The aggressive ones try to take over, the non-assertive ones retire into their shells and relinquish both their responsibilities and their rights. The all-action people want to push ahead with action (any action really, as long as **something** happens), while the more cautious, conservative members of the group dig their heels in and refuse to budge. Squabbles and even fierce arguments erupt. Dissension and discord stalk the corridors of power. No one is happy and not much useful work gets done (everyone is too busy Storming).

3 GROUP NORMING

This is when the group settle down and people begin to behave like the normal, rational individuals they really are. They begin to see each other as colleagues on the same side and, sometimes, even start to like one another. People begin to find ways of working together.

Routines and systems are established. People even begin to make allowances for others' habits and idiosyncrasies: 'We'll have to have a break 'cos you know Jim likes a cigarette halfway through'. Communication opens up, people relax and there is, generally, a little more laughter and light-heartedness.

Many groups stick at this stage and do not progress to stage 4, Performing. These groups do the job, more or less. There are, from time to time, hiccups and problems, but by and large people get on and get the job done.

4 GROUP PERFORMING

When teams begin to really Perform there is a marked difference in attitude and output. Every team member makes an appropriate contribution, using his or her knowledge and skills to the best of his or her ability. So if someone on the team is brilliant at making presentations – even though they hold a junior position within the organization, say – the team will **want** that person to present on the team's behalf. Status won't come into it. Susie is best for the job, so Susie does the job, because **it is best for the team**.

Team energy is high. There's a buzz around the team members. Ideas flow, everyone works hard, everyone is happy and willing to go the extra mile to get the results the team is looking for. There is a high level of respect on the team, for people and for the personal contribution each person makes. It doesn't matter that Paul couldn't be trusted to calculate the petty cash correctly – because he's brilliant at dealing with the press. Who cares if Lucy can't talk to clients – she's fantastic at organizing resources and making sure everyone meets their deadlines.

On a Performing team people trust one another, listen to and communicate with one another, reach decisions by consensus, help, co-operate and work together to finish the job on time, within budget, and to the very best of their ability.

How does this miraculous transition take place? What must occur to change people from behaving like truculent adolescents to confident individuals who are reaching and experiencing their full potential?

The answer lies in understanding:

- the roles people play on teams
- how to make the best use of each person's contribution
- the power of motivation

Summary

- The key attributes of a high performance team are:
  - alignment
  - co-operation
  - motivation
  - communication
  - positive response to external pressure

- Team alignment results when all the members of the team share a common:
  - vision
  - goal
  - strategy

- Team co-operation results when everyone on the team feels that:
  - the workload is shared equally
  - tasks are allocated in accordance with each person's strengths
  - no one is ever excluded because they hold a different view
  - everyone on the team is equal
  - everyone has the same information, at the same time
  - everyone has the same rights to contribute and communicate
  - everyone is treated in the same way

- Team communication results when people are encouraged to:
  - share ideas and express their opinions openly and honestly
  - tell each other what is going on – the bad as well as the good
  - trust and respect one another

- Team motivation results when people can see that they will receive positive rewards as a result of good teamwork

- Positive response to external pressure results when everyone on the team is committed to the team and the team's vision, objectives and strategy

- Any group of people who wish to become a high performance team must, naturally, progress through the four stages of:
  - Forming
  - Storming
  - Norming
  - Performing

- Group *forming* is the first stage of the process, when everyone is on their best behaviour. Internally people may be anxious; externally they are likely to be pleasant and eager to please, but also careful not to disclose too much. People with common interests or backgrounds may tend to gravitate towards one another and form sub-groups. There will be some jostling for position to get close to the team leader

- Group *storming* is the second stage of the process. There is resistance to control, resistance to the demands of the team's tasks and resistance to the team leader. Conflict arises between individual and individual, individual and sub-group and all other possible permutations. At this stage it looks as though the team may never be able to work together

- Group *norming* is the third stage of the process. People begin to settle down into their roles and tasks and start to behave **normally** towards one another. Routines and systems are established and communication improves. Many groups stick at the Norming stage

- Group *performing* is the fourth and final stage. People begin to see themselves as part of a cohesive unit – the team. Everyone wants what is best for the team, and team energy is high. Ideas and communication flow easily, and everyone wants to make a worthwhile contribution.

Note

1 Tuckman, B. (1965) 'Development Sequences in Small Groups', *Psychological Bulletin*.

Section 2 The roles people play

Introduction

People, at home and at work, function in different ways. Some are extrovert and need people, some are introvert and prefer their own company. Some are neat, tidy and highly organized, while others are careless, slapdash and highly disorganized. It doesn't mean that one is better than the other, although we often approve of those who are more like us, and disapprove of those who are not like us.

In this section of the Workbook we shall be looking at how different personality types approach work and how you can use that knowledge to get the very best out of the people on your team.

People differences

The rich variety of human nature is what makes relationships – at home and at work – so diverse, interesting, stimulating and, of course, challenging. Every individual has his or her own:

- likes and dislikes
- attitude and approaches
- values and beliefs
- speed of thought and action
- level of intelligence and creativity
- level of need for social interaction
- desire for risk and challenge, or – desire for stability and tranquillity

So in a team of three people you could find the following:

Lynn	Mike	Chris
■ Likes the countryside and enjoys a very quiet social life, preferring to spend time at home reading and sewing. Abhors television.	■ Likes sport and socializing with friends. Subscriber to Sky television and cheerfully admits he is addicted to watching late-night movies. Regular churchgoer.	■ Likes pubs and clubs and a varied and frenetic social life.
■ Lives with her partner of ten years	■ Married, two children	■ Single, lives alone, enjoys a variety of relationships while steering clear of commitment to any one person
■ Has been a member of the Liberal Democrat party for eight years	■ Used to be a member of Labour Militant	■ Votes Conservative at General Elections – otherwise totally disinterested in politics
■ Practising Buddhist	■ Committed Christian	■ Absolute atheist

They are all decent, intelligent, hard-working people, but they all have very different attitudes and approaches towards life. It doesn't mean that one person is right, making the other two wrong. It just means they are *different*.

In most cases, on teams, the one factor which people have in common is that **they are all different**. One of the keys to building a high performance team is to recognize and accept these differences, and to make them work for the good of the team.

The Cambridge psychologist, Meredith Belbin, has identified nine different roles which people play when working in a team situation. The term *team role* describes the way in which an individual will operate and function within a team and encompasses the way he or she:

- relates to the other team members
- communicates with the other team members
- contributes to the team

People don't say 'I will **choose**' this team role; they say 'I **fit** this team role description'. People don't say 'I would **like to be**' this team role; they say 'the description of this team role is a good description of **me**.'

The key to success is to:

1 **understand the differences between the individual people on the team** (what is this person like? how do they prefer to operate? what does he or she do best?)

2 **understand the differences between the team roles** (what strengths and

weaknesses does this role bring to the team? what does this team role contribute to the team?)

3 **allow people to operate in their own, natural team role strengths.** This is about allowing people to be themselves and to contribute to the team in the way that naturally suits them best. This is really fitting square pegs into square holes, and round pegs into round holes. When the *match* and *fit* are right, people will feel comfortable and at ease. They will feel they are making a genuine contribution to the team because their input will be **suited to their temperament and capabilities**.

Belbin's eight team roles are shown in Figure 2, below. **Note** Dr Belbin has also identified a ninth team role: that of the Specialist. The Specialist is someone who has an in-depth knowledge and understanding of their own (often narrow) field of interest and, usually, little interest in other topics. The role of the Specialist is described in detail in *Team Roles at Work* (1996), published by Butterworth-Heinemann.

```
1  Plant
2  Resource Investigator
3  Co-ordinator
4  Shaper
5  Monitor Evaluator
6  Team Worker
7  Implementer
8  Completer
```

Figure 2   Dr Meredith Belbin's eight team roles

The Plant

Someone who fits the description of Plant is:

- an ideas person. Their ideas are usually original, radical, imaginative, and *different*
- an intelligent person. They have a strong intellectual grasp of concepts and they like to tackle and solve complex, difficult problems
- an introverted person. They live inside their heads to a large extent, preferring to be caught up in their inner world of imagination and ideas, rather than the down-to-earth prosaic, real world of shopping and paying the bills and organizing family outings
- an unorthodox person. They prefer to work independently (rather than run with the herd), and they have an unconventional approach to life and relationships. If they are caught up in a knotty problem a Plant will appear at a

board meeting wearing laddered tights or the remains of last night's supper on their tie. Appearances and protocols are unimportant – the intellectual challenge is the thing

- their greatest contribution to the team is original thought, the ability to generate new and interesting ideas, and to solve complex problems
- their greatest failings are:
    - their ability (and desire) to live 'up in the clouds'
    - their inability to attend to detail (they prefer the big picture)
    - their sensitivity; they don't like criticism and have difficulty accepting praise
    - their inability to communicate easily with people who are not as bright or as unconventional as they are
- they are likely to say:
    'Give me a couple of days to think about this and I'll come up with a solution – I may need to work at home.'

The Resource Investigator

Someone who fits the description of Resource Investigator is:

- a people person. They need the stimulation of meeting and talking to others. They enjoy being out and about, networking with people away from the office, or communicating on the phone. They love to trawl for new ideas, or take an existing concept and expand it into something new and exciting
- an extrovert person. They are positive and optimistic, relaxed and gregarious, usually well liked and popular
- a diplomatic person. They are skilled negotiators who enjoy thinking on their feet and relish the challenge of working out a favourable deal
- an adventurous person. They respond well to challenges and cope admirably when under pressure.
- their greatest contribution to the team is energy, optimism and enthusiasm, which can help to motivate the other team members when the outlook is bleak and stormy
- their greatest failings are:
    - their lack of stamina. They can get very enthusiastic about something new, but, if unsupported by the rest of the team, they will quickly lose heart and move on to a better, more interesting, more exciting idea
    - their need for contact with people and for positive feedback
    - their tendency to be over optimistic: 'Hey, it'll be all right on the night!'
- they are likely to say:
    'Let me ask around – see what other people are doing to handle the situation. I'll make a few calls, meet a few people – get back to you.'

The Co-ordinator

Someone who fits the description of Co-ordinator is:

- a controlled and calm person. They have the ability to recognize other people's strengths and capabilities and then co-ordinate those elements for the good of the team
- a skilled communicator. They are adept at drawing out from each team member their views and opinions, and then summarizing and articulating the temperature and mood of the team
- a strong and steady person. They are calm and unflappable and often have a natural air of authority. When a crisis looms and a cool head is needed, the Co-ordinator is the person who can pull the team together
- a focused person. No matter what happens, they will help to keep the team focused on the tasks and activities which will lead towards achieving the desired outcome
- their greatest contribution to the team is their ability to unify the team and remind the team of the goals and objectives for which everyone is working so hard
- their greatest failings are:
  - their lack of creativity, zing and charisma
- they are likely to say:
  'Before we make a decision it's important that everyone has a chance to say how they feel about it.'

The Shaper

Someone who fits the description of Shaper is:

- a pushy person. They are extrovert, energetic, restless and, often, neurotic. They are results orientated, and will push and push to make things happen. They drive themselves hard – and drive everyone else on the team, too
- an impulsive person. They see something that needs to be done, and they will plunge straight in and do it – sometimes forgetting that consultation is part of the diplomatic process
- a thick-skinned person. They are able to work well in the midst of dissension and politically-charged atmospheres because they will just get on with their job, regardless of what is happening around them. Their ability to bulldoze their way through situations can often upset gentler, more sensitive team members
- their greatest contribution to the team is their ability to shape the team's efforts into a united and practical course of action, and then push ahead energetically to turn ideas into action and practical reality

- their greatest failings are:
    - their insensitivity to other people's feelings and needs
    - their ability to provoke, irritate and upset other people
- they are likely to say:
    'Oh, for goodness sake! We haven't got time for that – we need to get cracking now. Look, I'll just get on and do it … while you're thinking about it.'

The Monitor Evaluator

Someone who fits the description of Monitor Evaluator is:

- an analytical person. They are particularly good at examining ideas (often in exhaustive detail) to analyse the strengths and weaknesses of each, and then forming an opinion based on their findings
- a cautious, unemotional person. They don't have enthusiasms. They don't jump to conclusions. They don't act impulsively, or on instinct or gutfeeling
- a thorough person. A Monitor Evaluator will leave no stone unturned if asked to analyse and evaluate data. Other team members may be screaming for a decision, but the Monitor Evaluator will carefully, shrewdly and prudently weigh up all the pros and cons – no matter how long it takes
- a sober person. They find it hard to be optimistic and will see all the reasons why the team **should not** proceed with a course of action, and pay scant attention to the reasons why the team **should** act
- their greatest contribution to the team is their ability to take an objective view when considering other people's ideas. Often, a Monitor Evaluator will save the team from a rash and costly error of judgement
- their greatest failings are:
    - their lack of enthusiasm, and their inability to inspire or motivate their team members
    - their lack of tact and diplomacy; if they consider someone's cherished idea and it seems likely to end in tears, the Monitor Evaluator will say so, bluntly and directly, without any frills attached
- they are likely to say:
    'I'm not prepared to make a snap judgement. I want to look at all the angles before I make any kind of a decision.'

The Team Worker

Someone who fits the description of Team Worker is:

- a sociable person. They like people, and they like people to be happy together

- a loyal person. The team is really important to the Team Worker and they will work hard to preserve the team, and nurture team spirit, no matter how rocky the road becomes
- a diplomatic person. They are conscious of and concerned about the relationships within the team, and will make a real effort to pour oil on troubled waters when conflict occurs
- their greatest contribution to the team is their ability to support everyone, and keep the team functioning as smoothly and as harmoniously as is humanly possible
- their greatest failings are:
  - can be indecisive, particularly if they have to choose whether to put people and relationships first or tasks and objectives first
- they are likely to say:

  'Every story has more than one side – and everyone has a reason for behaving the way they do. The important thing to remember is that we're a team, and we have to stick together and help one another.'

The Implementer

Someone who fits the description of Implementer is:

- an organized person. They enjoy turning ideas into action and producing the goods on time, within budget
- a sensible, self-disciplined person. Implementers are good at turning chaos into order, and take pleasure in working out schedules and devising budgets, systems and procedures
- their greatest contribution to the team is their organizing ability and their skill at turning airy-fairy ideas into concrete plans of action
- their greatest failings are:
  - their inflexibility and resistance to change
- they are likely to say:

  'OK – before we do anything else we need to prepare a schedule, allocate responsibilities, set benchmarks and deadlines and create a system so that we can monitor progress.'

The Completer

Someone who fits the description of Completer is:

- an anxious person. Although they may appear to be cool, calm and collected, inwardly they are worried to death in case something goes wrong. Their strategy for reassuring themselves that nothing will go wrong is to check, re-check and then double-check all the details

■ A Completer **never** assumes it will be 'all right on the night'

■ a conscientious person. If a Completer says they will do something, then you can rely on the fact that not only will it be done, but it will be done on time, and to a very high standard

■ their greatest contribution to the team is their ability to take care of the details and to make sure that a project doesn't sink into oblivion just because one signature is missing from a contract, or an important telephone call is forgotten

■ their greatest failings are:
  – their high expectations of themselves **and** everyone else on the team.
  – their intolerance towards slapdash, careless, happy-go-lucky (and often highly creative) work

■ they are likely to say:
  'When the contracts are signed pass them to me so I can check them.'

The next activity, which is in two parts, will enable you to analyse which team role description best fits your own personality, and which team roles you have within your current team.

ACTIVITY 5

■ To determine which team role best describes your personality and operating style, consider the statements in each of the sections below. *Please note*: there are NO right or wrong answers, so take as much time as you need to answer each question honestly.

■ In each section, please choose up to THREE statements which most accurately describe how you operate and function (not how you would LIKE to operate and function).

■ When you have chosen your one, two or three statements, allocate 10 points between the statements, giving the most the points to the statement which is most accurate, and the least points to the statement which is least accurate.

Example 1

	Allocation of points
(a) I am outgoing, cheerful and enjoy socializing	
(b) I am introverted and inward-looking and generally prefer my own company	
(c) I have a small circle of close friends, all of whom I have known for some time (Yes – I suppose so)	1 point
(d) I have a wide circle of acquaintances, all of whom are very different	
(e) I enjoy meeting people, but time alone is very important to me (Yes! This is me)	7 points
(f) I have no more than five really important people in my life (Yes, this is true)	2 points

Allocation of points: 1 point + 7 points + 2 points = 10 points allocated between answers (c), (e) and (f)

Example 2

	Allocation of points
(a) I am outgoing, cheerful and enjoy socializing (Yes! This absolutely describes me – none of the other statements really apply to me)	10 points
(b) I am introverted and inward-looking and generally prefer my own company	
(c) I have a small circle of close friends, all of whom I have known for some time	
(d) I have a wide circle of acquaintances, all of whom are very different	
(e) I enjoy meeting people, but time alone is very important to me	
(f) I have no more than five really important people in my life	

Allocation of points: all 10 points allocated to answer (a)

Section 1 The main contribution I make to a team

Choose up to three statements which accurately describe you. Allocate a total of 10 points to your chosen statements.

		Allocation of points
(a)	I try to see and take advantage of new opportunities	
(b)	I enjoy working with people. Establishing and maintaining good working relationships are important to me	
(c)	I consider that my creativity is an important aspect of who I am, and my creativity is my most important contribution to any situation	
(d)	I have the ability to pull the team together when it looks as though we are in danger of forgetting our main objectives	
(e)	I am always concerned about the details, and prefer to leave the wider picture to other people	
(f)	I don't mind being temporarily unpopular as long as we get the job done	
(g)	I think my ability to get the team organized – and keep them organized – is my key contribution	
(h)	I am able to carefully assess a situation and calmly make an objective recommendation about the best course of action to take	

Section 2 My shortcomings when working in a team

Choose up to three statements which accurately describe you. Allocate a total of 10 points to your chosen statements.

		Allocation of points
(a)	I like things to be structured and ordered. I can't stand chaos and uncertainty	
(b)	It's important to me that everyone on the team has a chance to air their views – and I sometimes hold things up because I want to make sure everyone's ideas are properly considered	
(c)	I need support and positive feedback from the people I'm working with – if that isn't forthcoming, then I can lose interest in what the team is trying to achieve	
(d)	I can always see all the pros and cons – and people seem to think I enjoy pouring cold water on their off-the-wall ideas	
(e)	I tend to rub people up the wrong way – but when I see things that need to be done, it drives me crazy. I like to get on and do what's needed without messing around and wasting time	
(f)	I tend to be indecisive when I see the team splintering into different directions – I'm very sensitive to upset and atmosphere on the team	
(g)	I get so involved with new ideas that I can lose track of what's happening with other people on the team	
(h)	My concern over getting every detail right is upsetting for the more relaxed people on the team	

Section 3 When I'm working on a project with other people

Choose up to three statements which accurately describe you. Allocate a total of 10 points to your chosen statements.

	Allocation of points
(a) I focus on results – winning is important to me	
(b) Although I pay less attention to the big picture, my attention to detail helps the team avoid errors and omissions	
(c) I keep the team on track and on target so that we don't lose sight of our objectives	
(d) I work hard to make sure that my contribution is both creative and original	
(e) I like to encourage team spirit and a harmonious working atmosphere	
(f) I am always on the lookout for new ideas and developments which can help us	
(g) I bring objectivity and a cool head to the decision making process	
(h) I make sure that everything is properly organized – I feel that we need to get the systems right before we can move ahead	

Section 4 My usual approach to team work is ...

Choose up to three statements which accurately describe you. Allocate a total of 10 points to your chosen statements.

		Allocation of points
(a)	I like to get to know the people I'm working with	
(b)	I'm prepared to hold a minority view – if I think I'm right – and I'm happy to share my views with the rest of the team, even if the team sometimes feel that I am being challenging or difficult	
(c)	When I consider that the team is about to embark on an unsafe course of action, I am always able to prepare a logical and reasoned argument to prove my case	
(d)	I try to keep the team on course and steer people away from crazy, time-wasting, hare-brained ideas	
(e)	I expect a lot from myself, and from the people I'm working with	
(f)	I have no interest in getting involved in the politics of teamwork. If I'm to do my best work for the team, then I need time and space for myself	
(g)	I try to get everyone to see that the glass is 'half full', never 'half empty' – it's important to have a positive attitude and outlook	
(h)	I feel it's important to take a practical approach, and I try to ensure that everyone on the team is organized. Once we know what we have to do, how we're going to do it, and how we're to monitor it – then life becomes much easier	

Section 5 I enjoy job satisfaction when ...

Choose up to three statements which accurately describe you. Allocate a total of 10 points to your chosen statements.

	Allocation of points
(a) I have the time and opportunity to study the situation, carefully analyse all of the facts and then make a sound decision based on my analysis	
(b) I am able to find a practical solution to a problem, or bring order out of chaos	
(c) I feel that everyone is working well together and there is a strong sense of co-operation and camaraderie	
(d) I strongly influence the decision-making process	
(e) I have the opportunity to meet with people who have new ideas and perspectives which I can then offer to the team	
(f) I am instrumental in helping people to agree on a solution to a problem or on taking a specific course of action	
(g) I am able to focus all of my energy and attention on the job in hand	
(h) I have creative freedom	

Section 6   If I am suddenly asked to work on a difficult task with limited time and resources, and unfamiliar people ...

Choose up to three statements which accurately describe you. Allocate a total of 10 points to your chosen statements.

		Allocation of points
(a)	I would prefer to spend some time on my own to work out the best approach – and then take it from there	
(b)	I would spend some time trying to bring everyone together as a team, before we start work on the task	
(c)	I would begin by identifying what each person could best contribute to the task – their strengths and specialist skills	
(d)	I would set deadlines and targets – so that everyone would know what they had to do, and by when	
(e)	I would concentrate on staying cool, calm and collected so that the pressures would not interfere with my capacity to think logically	
(f)	I would focus on the task to be done, and would resist any attempts by anyone to cut corners, just because of the pressures of the situation	
(g)	I would lead from the front and give the team a clear sense of direction and purpose	
(h)	I would get everyone talking – that way we could stir up some new ideas and approaches	

Section 7 The main problems I experience when working on a team are ...

Choose up to three statements which accurately describe you. Allocate a total of 10 points to your chosen statements.

		Allocation of points
(a)	I get impatient and irritable with people who are slow to take action or reach a decision	
(b)	People think I'm too analytical and don't use my intuition or pay attention to gut-feelings	
(c)	People think I cause delays because I'm determined that things are done properly	
(d)	I get bored fairly quickly and, unless there are stimulating people on the team, I can lose interest in what's going on	
(e)	I don't respond well to criticism – especially if it comes from people who don't seem able to grasp my ideas	
(f)	People think I spend too much time getting a consensus of opinion before I take action	
(g)	People think I am rather narrow-minded and rigid in my thinking and my approaches	
(h)	I'm not very good at dealing with opposition or dissension, so, I'll give up on my ideas if it looks as though they could be a source of conflict	

FEEDBACK

1 Transfer the points you allocated in each section onto grid 1 below.

For example:

Example grid 1

	a	b	c	d	e	f	g	h
Section 1	7			2	1			
Section 2		3		6			1	
Section 3			5		4	1		
Section 4		3		3				4
Section 5	1		7		2			
Section 6		2	5			3		
Section 7				1			8	1

Your grid 1

	a	b	c	d	e	f	g	h
Section 1								
Section 2								
Section 3								
Section 4								
Section 5								
Section 6								
Section 7								

2 Now transfer your scores from grid 1 onto grid 2 below.

For example

Example grid 1

	a	b	c	d	e	f	g	h
Section 1	7			2	1			
Section 2		3		6			1	
Section 3			5		4	1		
Section 4		3		3				4
Section 5	1		7		2			
Section 6		2	5			3		
Section 7				1			8	1

Example grid 2

Section 1	c	a 7	d 2	f	h	b	g	e 1
Section 2	g 1	c	b 3	e	d 6	f	a	h
Section 3	d	f 1	c 5	a	g	e 4	h	b
Section 4	f	g	d 3	b 3	c	a	h 4	e
Section 5	h	e 2	f	d	a 1	c 7	b	g
Section 6	a	h	c 5	g	e	b 2	d	f 3
Section 7	e	d 1	f	a	b	h 1	g 8	c
Total	1	11	18	3	7	14	12	4
	Plant	R Invest.	Co-Ord.	Shaper	M-Eval.	Team W	Implem.	Comp.[1]

This person:

■ usually operates as a Co-ordinator – score 18
■ can operate as a Team Worker - score 14
■ can also operate as a Implementer - score 12

Transfer your allocations from grid 1 onto grid 2 below.

Your grid 2

Section 1	c	a	d	f	h	b	g	e
Section 2	g	c	b	e	d	f	a	h
Section 3	d	f	c	a	g	e	h	b
Section 4	f	g	d	b	c	a	h	e
Section 5	h	e	f	d	a	c	b	g
Section 6	a	h	c	g	e	b	d	f
Section 7	e	d	f	a	b	h	g	c
Total								
	Plant	R -Invest.	Co-Ord.	Shaper	M -Eval.	Team W	Implem.	Comp.

Finally, total your scores:

■ Your highest score will give you your preferred team role. This is the role you usually adopt when functioning as part of a team; the role which reflects your personality and style
■ Your next two highest scores will give you the other roles which you are able to adopt within a team, if necessary
■ You should notice that people almost never operate solely and exclusively in a single role. People have repertoires of behaviours, strengths and weaknesses, and these, too, should be acknowledged and recognized.

The next activity will give you an opportunity to think about the members of your team, and the roles they naturally adopt in a team situation.

ACTIVITY 6

You may need to photocopy the chart below, so that you have one blank chart for each member of your team. For each person, tick the words which, in your opinion, best describe how that person functions and operates as a team member.
For example:

Name: Carolyn						
I	2	3	4	5	6	7
Impatient	Kind	Cold	Emotional	Sensitive	Direct	Careful

NAME:						
I	2	3	4	5	6	7
Impatient	Kind	Cold	Emotional	Sensitive	Sensible	Careful
8	9	10	11	12	13	14
Independent	Outgoing	Steady	Neurotic	Cautious	Perfectionist	Adventurous
15	16	17	18	19	20	21
Inflexible	Sociable	Indecisive	Logical	Insensitive	Unorthodox	Cordial
22	23	24	25	26	27	28
Objective	Impulsive	Eccentric	Organized	Optimistic	Loner	Supportive
29	30	31	32	33	34	35
Sensible	Ambitious	Extrovert	Introvert	Diplomatic	Fussy	Analytical
36	37	38	39	41	41	42
Thorough	Intellectual	Loyal	Practical	Anxious	Forceful	Co-operative
43	44	45	46	47	48	49
Restless	Calm	Enthusiastic	Networker	Blunt	Unflappable	Pushy
50	51	52	53	54	55	56
Soothing	Sober	Obsessive	Self-disciplined	Independent	Cheerful	Focused

FEEDBACK

For each person for whom you have completed a chart, note down the numbers you have ticked, and then compare them against the lists below.

Again, the highest score or number of ticks will reflect the team member's usually preferred team role.

Plant numbers: 5, 8, 20, 24, 27, 32, 37, 54

Team strengths: intelligence, ideas, creativity, originality
Team weaknesses: introverted, not really a team player, independent, unconventional, needs careful handling

Resource Investigator numbers: 9, 14, 16, 26, 31, 45, 46, 55

Team strengths: outgoing, optimistic, excellent at networking and gathering new contacts, new ideas
Team weaknesses: easily bored, not much stamina, dislike of detail, needs people as a stimulus

Co-ordinator numbers: 10, 21, 29, 33, 44, 48, 56

Team strengths: diplomatic, calm, capable of keeping the team focused on the job in hand
Team weaknesses: can be seen as aloof or authoritarian, usually not especially intelligent or creative

Shaper numbers: 1, 4, 11, 19, 23, 30, 41, 43, 49

Team strengths: can galvanize the team into action, enthusiastic, energetic, hard-working
Team weaknesses: bossy, insensitive to other people's feelings, undiplomatic, unthinking. Will do whatever it takes to achieve desired results or fulfil personal ambitions.

Monitor Evaluator numbers: 3, 18, 22, 35, 36, 47

Team strengths: unemotional, analytical, capable of making objective decisions, able to see all the plus and minus factors in any situation
Team weaknesses: lack of humour, lack of enthusiasm, inability to motivate others.

Teamworker numbers: 2, 17, 28, 38, 42, 50, 55

Team strengths: loyalty, concern for the team and relationships within the team; will make great efforts to hold the team together and promote unity and harmony.
Team weaknesses: lack of imagination and drive, tendency to put people before objectives or results

Implementer numbers: 12, 15, 25, 39, 53

Team strengths: organization, self-discipline, single-mindedness, capable of systematically turning concepts and ideas into working systems and procedures
Team weaknesses: can be inflexible, narrow-minded and very resistant to change

Completer numbers: 7, 13, 34, 40, 52

Team strengths: conscientious, meticulous attention to detail, extremely high standards; capacity for relentless follow-through will ensure that tasks are carried through to a successful conclusion
Team weaknesses: inability to delegate, intolerance of less than perfect work from others, high anxiety

Strengths and weaknesses

Each of the eight team roles discussed so far has its own particular strengths which can make a strong, positive contribution to the team.

Watch out for excess, because when this happens, the strengths metamorphose into weaknesses, with a consequent negative effect on the team. Some examples of this are given in Figure 3 below.

Strength	Excess leads to
Trust is a strength which enables people to count on others to do the right thing	**Gullibility** – believing what anyone says without checking and verifying the facts
Optimism is a strength which enables people to feel that everything will turn out for the best	**Impracticality** – wanting things to work out and hoping that things will work out, and not recognizing when things are going wrong
Loyalty is a strength which enables people to support their friends and colleagues through thick and thin	**Unethical behaviour** – being so loyal to friends and colleagues that unethical or unprofessional conduct is ignored
Influencing skills are a strength which enables people to persuade others to see their point of view	**Pressurizing behaviour** – exerting undue pressure on others to conform to certain views or take certain actions
Thoroughness is a strength which enables people to do things properly and completely	**Obsession** – being so concerned that things are done thoroughly that the behaviour becomes compulsive
Independence is a strength which enables people to work alone and use their initiative	**Isolation** – being so concerned to retain autonomy that people distance themselves and isolation results
Ambition is a strength which enables people to develop their careers, their life style, their prospects for the future	**Ruthlessness** – being so ambitious that other people's needs and feelings are totally ignored in the rush to climb the ladder to success
Self-confidence is a strength which enables people to tackle most situations	**Arrogance** – being so confident that other people's opinions aren't worth listening to

Figure 3   How strengths can become weaknesses

The perfect team

In an ideal world, a perfect team would consist of at least eight people, each of whom would be comfortable operating in one of Belbin's eight team roles. This perfect mix is highly unlikely. In fact, you are much more likely to find teams composed of highly unsatisfactory combinations, such as:

- three Shapers and one Plant
- two Monitor Evaluators, two Completers and one Team Worker
- four Resource Investigators and one Monitor Evaluator
- three Plants and one Implementer

You might like to speculate (using Figure 3 as a reference) what kinds of dysfunctional behaviours might occur in each of the examples above. Have you seen any teams with these behaviours?

Sometimes teams are brought together by circumstance or practicality, rather than best practice. If you are given a team of people, then you simply have to work with the individuals and seek to make the best of what you have got.

If you are lucky enough to be able to hand-pick a team for a specific project, then Dr Meredith Belbin has some suggestions as to how you can create a good, if not perfect, mix of people. Dr. Belbin suggests that the six key factors which are most likely to influence whether or not a team performs well are:

- **the chair person**
  The person who chairs important team discussions should, ideally, be someone fairly senior who fits the Co-ordinator profile. (This does not have to be the team leader.)
- **a Plant**
  Every successful team needs one Plant. One is the optimum number. More than one Plant is a minus factor because they will get too involved in criticizing and judging each other's ideas.
- **a good spread of mental abilities**
  Ideally there should be one very clever team member, plus one person who is sufficiently clever to stimulate and challenge the really clever person. In addition, there should also be some team members who are not bright enough to get involved in the really clever discussions. Dr. Belbin suggests that the less clever people, unable to compete intellectually, will look around for other, more fulfilling roles which they can handle on the team.
- **as wide a spread of team roles as is possible**
  Ideally, one of each.
- **a match between individual's attributes and the work that is allocated to them**
  Sometimes this may mean disregarding experience or seniority, but the key factor is matching tasks to individual preferences and capabilities. For example, the Resource Investigator may be the most senior person, but they are not the best person to prepare the budgets and schedules. The

Plant may be the most experienced person, but they are not the best person to make an important presentation to a new client.

■ Recognition of imbalance in the team and the ability to adjust to it
The most successful teams are those which recognise any imbalances within the team and are prepared to adapt or change roles in order to compensate for team strengths and weaknesses.[2]

Margerison and McCann

Charles Margerison and Dick McCann have developed a *team management wheel* which outlines team roles in a way which is not dissimilar to Belbin's work.[3]

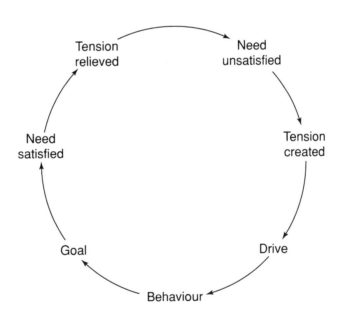

Figure 4

MARGERISON AND McCANN TEAM ROLES:

■ *Reporter Advisers* provide a support role in the organization, and collect and disseminate information and resources

■ *Creator Innovators* enjoy thinking up new ideas and put a lot of effort into experimenting with and designing new approaches and ways of doing things

■ *Explorer Promoters* go out and publicize new ideas and bring in new resources and contacts

■ *Assessor Developers* identify how ideas will work in practice and like to assess the viability of proposals

■ *Thruster Organizers* favour an organizing role. They put the pressure on so that systems are created, procedures for work allocation are organized, and they make sure that time and output targets are set

■ *Concluder Producers* follow through on the work of other team members and set high standards for service or product

■ *Controller Inspectors* inspect work and ensure that jobs are done correctly

■ *Upholder Maintainers* maintain physical resources as well as social and organizational systems and relationships

■ *Linkers* play a key role by co-ordinating and integrating the others on the team. (The Linker may or may not be the team leader.)

Areas of conflict

On a perfect team, in an ideal world, not only would you have 'one of each', but all of these individuals would work together harmoniously and joyfully, with never a hint of a disagreement, let alone a cross word. Maybe there is some alternative universe where this happens, but here, in the real world, this state of affairs is as unlikely as a British heatwave at Christmas.

Because each of the eight team types is so fundamentally different, there is bound to be considerable potential for conflict. The next activity will give you an opportunity to consider how the conflict might occur, and between whom.

ACTIVITY 7

For the purpose of this activity imagine that, on your team, there are eight people, each one of whom is naturally one of Belbin's eight team types. Who is most likely to clash with whom, and why? Complete the chart below:

Team role	Most likely to come into conflict with which other team role(s)?	Most likely reasons for conflict
Plant		
Resource Investigator		
Co-ordinator		
Shaper		
Monitor Evaluator		
Team Worker		
Implementer		
Completer		

FEEDBACK

Some (although not all) potential areas of conflict between team roles are shown in the chart below.

Team role	Most likely to come into conflict with which other team role(s)?	Most likely reasons for conflict
Plant	Team Worker Shaper	Introverted Plants are often not particularly good team players and may not be keen to socialize. Plants can find the Shaper's relentless energy and ambition just too much to take
Resource investigator	Monitor Evaluator Completer	Resource Investigators are outgoing, optimistic people who can usually see all of the advantages and none of the snags. Dry, unemotional, analytical Monitor Evaluators tend to pour cold water on Resource Investigators' bright ideas. Resource Investigators are not strong on detail, and the Completer's obsession with getting things right can cause the Resource Investigator to quickly lose interest
Co-ordinator	Team Worker	Co-ordinators are focused people and objectives are important to them. They can clash with Team Workers who put relationships top of the agenda, and objectives and results lower down
Shaper	Anyone who doesn't see things their way	Monitor Evaluators set great store by objectivity, and can find the Plant's creative, unorthodox approach unnerving
Team Worker	Will make a real effort to get on with everyone and maintain harmony	Implementers, with their love of schedules, budgets, systems and procedures, can find the outgoing, extrovert RI upsetting, and the absent-minded, unorthodox Plant completely incomprehensible
Completer	Anyone and everyone who takes even a vaguely relaxed approach to the team, its tasks and its objectives	

Ways in which you can attempt to minimize conflict and maintain harmony on the team include:

- **Identify most likely areas of potential conflict.** Work out who you have on the team, and who is most likely to conflict with whom. Then separate the people who are most likely to clash. You can do this by sub-dividing the team into different sub-teams or working parties, each with responsibility for a different aspect of the project. In addition, try to ensure that at team meetings where everyone is present, you also have a Team Worker or Co-ordinator to keep the peace.

- **Reshuffle with another team or recruit.** This may involve talking to another team who has, say, two Plants, and who is prepared to swop a Plant for a Team Worker or a Completer. If this isn't feasible or possible, you may have to recruit a particular team role to join the team. Your *person specification* should clearly profile the team role for which you are looking. (Person specifications are covered in detail in Workbook 11, *Getting the Right People to do the Right Job*).

- **Allocate the right kinds of work to the appropriate team roles.** Make sure that you allocate tasks according to skills, abilities and Team Role preferences. For example, don't ask the Plant to monitor the budget; don't expect the Resource Investigator to work alone in isolated splendour; don't ask the Shaper to undertake an especially tricky and sensitive negotiation with someone for whom he or she has scant respect.

Work allocations

Understanding the roles that people naturally assume on teams is extremely helpful when you are allocating work to individual team members.

If you have a larger team with a wide spread of team roles, then it is worth taking the likes and dislikes of each individual team role into account.

PLANTS

Work best when they:

- work alone at their own pace, in their own way
- work in an informal, liberal, unstructured environment where protocol and company politics are low down on the agenda
- don't have to socialize or mix with too many people outside the team

RESOURCE INVESTIGATORS

Work best when they:

- have the freedom to get out and about, meeting people, making new contacts, gathering ideas from a number of different sources
- work with other people, not alone
- don't have to spend time working on the details

CO-ORDINATORS

Work best when they:

- know exactly what it is that the team, as a whole, and they, as individuals, are supposed to achieve
- have the opportunity to work with other people and encourage them to contribute the most appropriate skills and qualities to the team effort
- don't have to work in a highly intuitive or creative way

SHAPERS

Work best when they:

- have sufficient authority to use their initiative, make decisions and work at their own speed (which is usually quite fast)
- are allowed to do things their way
- don't have to compromise too much or run with the herd

MONITOR EVALUATORS

Work best when they:

- have time to think things through and consider all the angles
- have all the facts and relevant information before they make a decision
- aren't expected to motivate others, or to be the life and soul of the party

TEAM WORKERS

Work best when they:

- have the time and opportunity to create strong links and good working relationships with the other people on the team
- are allowed to support and encourage team members, and take the time to build team spirit
- don't like have to take sides or make decisions which might cause upset on the team

IMPLEMENTERS

Work best when they:

- operate in an organized environment
- are allowed to schedule and prioritize, allocate responsibilities and time-frames, set benchmarks and deadlines
- don't have to work in a slapdash, haphazard way, or with people who play it by ear and think on their feet

COMPLETERS

Work best when they:

- have the opportunity check and double-check all the details
- are able to see a job through to its completion
- they don't cope well with leaving things to chance, hoping for the best or keeping their fingers crossed

Often teams consist of fewer than eight people – maybe just two or three individuals to perform all of the tasks and bring the project to a successful conclusion on time. If you have a small team – say, just three people – then the allocation of work will have to be made on the basis of:

- **What is there to do?**
  What is involved? Are there numerous, complex tasks?
  One large, but fairly straightforward task?
  How many people will be needed to complete each task?
  Will the team achieve better results if more than one person is involved?
- **Who is capable of doing it?**
  Who has the necessary skills, abilities and experience?
  Who has done something similar before? Who would enjoy it the most? Would the person who would derive the most pleasure and satisfaction from undertaking the task bring the most energy and enthusiasm to the task?
- **Who has the time?**
  Who is available, in terms of time? Who can commit themselves to completing this task?
- **Who needs the development?**
  Who has never done something similar before and might benefit from undertaking this task as a development opportunity?
  How would this affect team results?

The next activity will give you an opportunity to clarify the way in which you normally allocate tasks to individual members of your current team.

ACTIVITY 8   C13

Read through the outline project below and then complete the chart below by allocating appropriate tasks to the **existing members of your current team**, giving the reasons for your choices.

Outline project
- Devise a new product for a European market
- Agree specification for product and packaging
- Negotiate supplier contracts
- Negotiate production schedules
- Assess competitive advantage and market position
- Identify pricing strategy
- Prepare budgets, schedules, deadlines
- Create a marketing strategy
- Select a marketing company to run the advertising campaign
- Monitor progress
- Launch the product

Task allocation	Existing team member's name preferred team role	Reason for allocating this task to this team member

Summary

- The psychologist Dr Meredith Belbin has identified eight team roles which people adopt when they become part of a team

- People cannot choose the team role they **naturally** adopt, although they can choose – when necessary – to adopt a secondary team role which fits their style, temperament and personality

- The eight team roles are the:
    - Plant
    - Resource Investigator
    - Co-ordinator
    - Shaper
    - Monitor Evaluator
    - Team Worker
    - Implementer
    - Completer

- Key features of the Plant:
    - intelligent, creative, original, independent
    - can be introverted and unconventional, not naturally a team player
    - work best on their own

- Key features of the Resource Investigator:
    - outgoing, optimistic and excellent at networking, making new contacts, gathering new ideas
    - easily bored, can quickly lose enthusiasm for a project unless stimulated by people and positive feedback
    - work best when they have freedom to get out and about and meet people

- Key features of the Co-ordinator:
    - diplomatic, calm and capable. Keep the team focused on the team's objectives
    - can be seen as aloof and not one of the gang
    - work best when they know what the team is supposed to achieve and what, precisely, their own objectives are

- Key features of the Shaper:
    - enthusiastic, energetic, hard-working, spring into action and can be the driving force which pushes the team forward
    - can be bossy and overbearing. Will do whatever it takes to achieve results – even if that means upsetting the team
    - work best when they can use their own initiative and they don't have to compromise too much

- Key Features of the Monitor Evaluator:
  - unemotional, analytical, capable of making objective decisions based on the facts alone
  - can lack humour and enthusiasm, and invariably think they are 'right'
  - work best when they are allowed time to analyse all the facts

- Key Features of the Team Worker:
  - loyalty towards and concern for the team
  - tendency to put people and relationships before objectives or results
  - work best when they have the time and the freedom to create good working relationships with the other team members

- Key features of the Implementer:
  - organization and the ability to turn ideas into practical action
  - can be inflexible and rigid in outlook, often very resistant to change
  - work best when they are allowed to work in a very organized way

- Key features of the Completer:
  - meticulous attention to detail and high standards, both for self and others
  - unwillingness to delegate, intolerance of less than 'perfect' work, anxiety and obsessive behaviour
  - work best when they are allowed to check and double-check everything – other people's work as well as their own

- The Charles Margerison and Dick McCann team roles:
  - Reporter Adviser
  - Creator Innovator
  - Explorer Promoter
  - Assessor Developer
  - Thruster Organizer
  - Concluder Producer
  - Controller Inspector
  - Upholder Maintainer
  - Linker

- You can minimize conflict between individuals operating in different team roles by:
  - identifying the people who are most likely to come into conflict and assigning those people to different working parties or sub-groups
  - ensuring that you have a Team Worker or Co-ordinator available to keep the peace on the team
  - filling as many of the team roles as possible, so that there is a group spread of types and capabilities
  - allocating the right kind of tasks to each team role

- When allocating work, always consider:
  - What is there to do?
  - Who is capable of doing it?
  - Who has the time?
  - Who needs the development?

Notes

1 Plant, Resource-Investigator, Co-ordinator, Shaper, Monitor Evaluator, Team Worker, Implementer, Completer

2 Jay, Ros (1995) *Build A Great Team*, Institute of Management and Pitman Publishing.

3 Margerison, Charles and McCann, Dick (1985) *How to Lead a Winning Team*, MCB University Press.

Section 3
Motivation

Introduction

Motivation is the driving force which makes us **want** to do things **willingly and well.**

If we are **not** motivated, we do things grudgingly, half-heartedly, carelessly. We go through the motions because we know we have to do it, but we don't really care about the end result. If we **are** motivated, then we **willingly** expend time, energy, thought and resources to achieve the positive end result we **desire.** It's the difference between:

- inviting the neighbours to dinner (something out of the chill cabinet with a bottle of plonk) because it's our turn and we can't get out of it
  and
- inviting good friends to dinner (a lovingly prepared menu with a couple of bottles of really good wine) because we want to see them and spend time with them
- approaching writing a report with dread and boredom – before we've even started the job – and producing the bare minimum
  and
- approaching writing a report with energy and enthusiasm and producing a document which is well researched and logically presented

In this section of the Workbook we'll be examining three theories which seek to explain precisely what it is that motivates most people.

Motivating your team

Building a high performance team depends, to a large extent, on:

- understanding what motivation is and how it works
- recognizing the motivators which each individual on the team responds to best
- working out how you can apply the appropriate motivators to encourage someone to work **willingly** and **well**

Amount of motivation = Amount of effort expended
High motivation = High effort
Low motivation = Low effort

Figure 5   Motivation is what makes people do things willingly and well

There are many theories about motivation. We will pay attention to three of the most well known:

- Theory X and Theory Y
- Hygiene factors
- Hierarchy of needs

and it is important to understand the basic assumptions which underpin each of them.

McGregor's Theory X and Theory Y

Professor Douglas McGregor devised the concept that managers are either 'Theory X' managers or 'Theory Y' managers. 'X' and 'Y' managers make different assumptions about the people they work with, and those assumptions affect how they manage their people. The activity which follows will give you an opportunity to check out some of your assumptions.

ACTIVITY 1

Consider each of the statements below and tick the statement which most accurately reflects your personal view.

1a People are basically dishonest	❏
1b People are basically honest	❏
2a People are not prepared to take responsibility	❏
2b People enjoy taking responsibility	❏
3a People are basically lazy and dislike work	❏
3b People enjoy working and achieving	❏
4a People cannot be trusted to work on their own	❏
4b People often produce the best results when they are left alone and trusted to get on with the job	❏
5a People need to know what the consequences will be if they do not produce good results	❏
5b People are more likely to respond to a carrot, rather than to a stick	❏
6a People need discipline and control	❏
6b People work best when they have freedom to use their own initiative and judgement	❏

FEEDBACK

- 1a, 2a, 3a, 4a, 5a, 6a are 'Theory X' responses.
- 1b, 2b, 3b, 4b, 5b, 6b are 'Theory Y' responses.

The difference between these two approaches is shown in Figure 6 below.

Theory X managers have little regard for people, tend to be very authoritarian and, generally, are highly unlikely to be able to motivate anyone to work **willingly** and **well**. **Theory Y** managers take a quite different view – believing that people are capable of undertaking responsible and creative work and accepting that people will work **willingly** and **well** providing that they understand and are committed to whatever it is they are doing. For example:

Theory X managers	**Theory Y managers**
The people under me are hapless, helpless and hopeless. If I don't keep on top of them, nothing will get done. I can't trust them to work on their own or do anything unless they are closely supervised and monitored. They have to know what will happen to them if they don't perform! I don't trust them.	The people on my team are individuals with individual skills and capabilities. Each one wants to do well, and part of my task is to ensure that everyone on the team has the opportunity to expand and develop their skills. They all know what is expected of them, and they are all committed to achieving the team's objectives. I trust them.

Managers who take a Theory X approach to managing subordinates believe that people:	**Managers who take a Theory Y approach to managing subordinates believe that people:**
■ have an inherent dislike of work and will avoid it whenever they can ■ are intrinsically lazy and need to be pushed and prodded before they will accept responsibility or make a contribution ■ must be coerced, controlled, pushed, directed and threatened with punishment if results are to be achieved ■ resist change, on principle ■ are easily fooled	■ enjoy challenging and interesting work ■ will use imagination, creativity and ingenuity to solve work problems – if they are given the opportunity ■ will accept responsibility and will exercise self-direction and self-control ■ will actively seek to develop their skills and abilities to achieve objectives which they find meaningful and to which they are committed ■ are not naturally lazy – it's how they are treated at work which makes them act that way

Figure 6   Theory X and Theory Y

Increasingly, in the 1990s, there are not too many Theory X managers around. They have either lost their jobs as the result of a downsizing exercise, or they have shifted to the Theory Y viewpoint because **Theory Y managers consistently achieve better results**.

Herzberg and the hygiene factors

In the early 1960s in the USA Frederick Herzberg devised his Motivation Hygiene Theory.

Herzberg researched motivation by asking people two questions:

■ What are the factors which contribute to your satisfaction with your work?
■ What are the factors that demotivate you at work?

A clear pattern emerged from his research.

HERZBERG'S MOTIVATORS (THE FACTORS WHICH CONTRIBUTED TO PEOPLE'S SATISFACTION AT WORK)

- *Security.* People want to feel secure:
  - in their job, without having to worry about whether they will get the sack, be made redundant or unexpectedly lose their freelance contract
  - in their ability to do the job, and their competence to handle most situations which might occur
  - that their line manager or team leader will support them, and will not show them up or cause them to lose face in front of others
- *Interest.* People want to be able to:
  - use their existing skills and knowledge and, where possible, acquire new ones
  - take a measure of responsibility, use their initiative, be involved in the decision-making process
  - do a good job and take pride in the quality of their work
- *Recognition.* People need to:
  - recognize the value of the work they are doing
  - gain respect from the people they work with and from family, friends and society as a whole
- *Advancement.* People need to be able to:
  - move up to more important, more complex, more responsible, more challenging work

HERZBERG'S HYGIENE FACTORS (THOSE FACTORS WHICH CAUSED PEOPLE TO BE DISSATISFIED WITH THEIR WORK)

- money
- hours of work
- holidays
- pension rights
- health care provision
- parking and canteen facilities
- office space and furniture
- range of technological 'toys' supplied (laptops, mobile phones, etc.)

Herzberg argues that:

- people achieve *job satisfaction* through the motivators
- people suffer *job dissatisfaction* because of the hygiene factors

Herzberg used the term *hygiene factors* because of the similarity between his line of thinking and initiatives in public health. For example:

- an efficient sewerage system does not make sick people well, but it does help to prevent cholera

■ a clear water system does not make sick people well, but it does help to prevent typhoid

Accordingly, in line with Herzberg's theory, to motivate your people you need to:

■ provide security, interest, recognition and advancement to motivate people to work willingly and well
■ make sure that the hygiene factors – pay, hours, holidays, etc. – are sufficiently attractive so as not to cause people to be dissatisfied with their jobs

Maslow's hierarchy of needs

The psychologist Abraham Maslow created the model of 'The Five Most Important Needs'. These needs are shown in Figure 7 below.

Figure 7   Maslow's hierarchy of needs

The next activity will give you an opportunity to consider how we are motivated when these needs are met, and demotivated when these needs are not met.

ACTIVITY 10

Read through the case study below and identify, in the right-hand column:
- ■ which one of the five basic needs is met, and how this might act as a motivator
- ■ which one of the five basic needs is not met, and how this might act as a demotivator

CASE STUDY

Charles is a senior manager with Bardon Plastics. He has been informed by his CEO that he and his team must present themselves at 7 a.m. at Kielder Forest for an 'Outdoor Training and Team Building Event' on Monday 21 October.

At 6 a.m. on the 21 Charles sets off, somewhat reluctantly, to the outdoor training centre. In his haste, he forgets that he has been advised to dress warmly for the occasion, so he is wearing a lightweight sweater and a golfing jacket.

Having underestimated the travelling time, Charles is the last person to arrive. Consequently, all of the waterproof clothing has been distributed and Charles is given the very last pair of wellington boots, size 7 – two sizes smaller than he normally wears.

The course leader explains that the first team task is to build a raft and cross a narrow, but fast-flowing river.

By 8.30 a.m. it is raining hard, and Charles is soaked to the skin. He's cold, wet, his feet hurt, and he is generally deeply unhappy.

By 9.15 a.m. the raft is completed and its time for the team to test whether their contraption will carry them across the water to the other bank. As Charles can't swim he is

Basic need? Met or not met? Is Charles demotivated?

horrified when the course leader cheerfully tells them 'Hang on tight, but if you come off, just swim like hell to the other side.'

At 9.30am, safely on dry land once again, Charles is chosen to act as team leader for the next exercise. The activity, which involves rope-knotting, bridge-building and similar feats of engineering, is way beyond Charles' capabilities. (He achieved a First in Economics at Cambridge and has never, ever, been a Boy Scout.) As the activity progresses he finds that he is being side-lined by the team, who realize that he doesn't have a clue. The team look for leadership to Dave, a highly practical individual with experience of marine engineering. No one listens to Charles when he makes a tentative suggestion, and he quickly realizes that he has been 'dumped' and is now operating on the periphery of the team. The completed bridge is a huge success, and Dave is warmly congratulated by everyone.

At 12 noon, to Charles' relief, everyone takes a break inside for lunch.

After lunch the team is taken, blindfolded, to a man-made maze set in the heart of the forest. The blindfolds are removed and the team is given thirty minutes to work out how to get to the exit. The team splits into dissenting factions as no one can agree on the best approach. Matters are made worse when Sylvia admits that she is claustrophobic and she is beginning to panic.

Charles, who is fond of puzzles and intellectual games, thinks he may have the solution. He explains his idea to the team and, within twenty minutes, Charles triumphantly leads the team through the twisting turns to the exit of the maze where the course leader is waiting.

Basic need? Met or not met? Is Charles demotivated?

CASE STUDY

Charles is a senior manager with Bardon Plastics. He has been informed by his CEO that he and his team must present themselves at 7 a.m. at Kielder Forest for an 'Outdoor Training and Team Building Event' on Monday 21st October.

At 6am on the 21st Charles sets off, somewhat reluctantly, to the outdoor training centre. In his haste, he forgets that he has been advised to dress warmly for the occasion, so he is wearing a lightweight sweater and a golfing jacket.

Having underestimated the travelling time, Charles is the last person to arrive. Consequently, all of the waterproof clothing has been distributed and Charles is given the very last pair of wellington, size 7 – two sizes smaller than he normally wears.

The course leader explains that the first team task is to build a raft and cross a narrow, but fast-flowing river.

By 8.30 a.m. it is raining hard and Charles is soaked to the skin. He's cold, wet, his feet hurt and he generally deeply unhappy.

> - Basic **Physical** need **not** met
>   Because he is cold, wet and his feet hurt, Charles' **number one priority** is to get warm, dry and comfortable. He is not in the least motivated to build a raft and cross a fast-flowing river. He is, however, highly motivated to get inside, out of the cold, dry off and remove the too-small wellingtons. That's all he's interested in. No one will be able to motivate him to do **anything** until his basic physical needs are met.

By 9.15 a.m. the raft is completed, and it's time for the team to test whether their contraption will carry them across the water to the other bank. As Charles can't swim he is horrified when the course leader cheerfully tells them: 'Hang on tight, but if you come off, just swim like hell to the other side'.

> - Basic **Security** need **not** met
>   Charles is scared – he can't swim and it seems to him as though he could be in danger of drowning. His **number one priority** at this point in time is his safety and security. He is not interested in how well the team performs because he is too concerned about **what is going to happen to him**. Will he survive? Will he make it to the other side?

At 9.30 a.m., safely on dry land once again, Charles is chosen to act as team leader for the next exercise. The activity, which involves rope-knotting, bridge-building and similar feats of engineering, is way beyond Charles' capabilities. (He achieved a First in Economics at Cambridge and has never, ever, been a Boy Scout.) As the activity progresses he finds that he is being side-lined by the team, who realize that he doesn't have a clue.

> ■ Basic **Self-esteem** need **not** met
>
> Charles is a senior manager – but he feels as though he's let the team down. He feels embarrassed by his lack of knowledge and skills, and worried that the team will lose respect for him. His confidence takes a nose-dive and so does his motivation: 'I can't do this – so there's no point in trying anyway … and it's a pointless exercise … complete waste of time.'

The team looks for leadership to Dave, a highly practical individual with experience of marine engineering. No one listens to Charles when he makes a tentative suggestion and he quickly realizes that he has been 'dumped' and is now operating on the periphery of the team. The completed bridge is a huge success, and Dave is warmly congratulated by everyone.

> ■ Basic **Social** need **not** met
>
> Charles recognizes that he has not only been displaced by Dave, but he is also not really accepted as part of the group. He feels rejected, unwelcome and uncomfortable. Because he doesn't feel part of what is going on, he is not motivated to make a contribution.

At 12 noon, to Charles' relief, everyone takes a break inside for lunch.

> ■ Basic **Physical** need **is** met
>
> As soon as Charles has the opportunity to get warm, dry out and have something to eat, he begins to feel better. He can stop worrying about how awful he feels and start thinking about what is going to happen next. His motivation to make a positive contribution increases.

After lunch the team is taken, blindfolded, to a man-made maze set in the heart of the forest. The blindfolds are removed and the team is given thirty minutes to work out how to get to the exit. The team splits into dissenting factions as no-one can agree on the best approach. Matters are made worse when Sylvia admits that she is claustrophobic and she is beginning to panic.

Charles, who is fond of puzzles and intellectual games, thinks he may have the solution. He explains his idea to the team and, within twenty minutes, Charles triumphantly leads the team through the twisting turns to the exit of the maze where the course leader is waiting.

> ■ Basic **Social** need **is** met
>
> As people listen to him, Charles begins to feel accepted by the team. He is motivated to do well and recover his credibility after the morning's fiasco.

> ■ Basic **Self-esteem** need **is** met
>
> Charles is aware that he is making a positive contribution. Because the team appreciate his efforts his self-esteem is restored and his confidence soars. He really wants to lead the team out of the maze … and he believes he can do it. His motivation is high.

■ Basic **Self-actualization** need **is** met

Through his successful leadership during the maze activity he has been able to demonstrate his knowledge, intellectual ability and leadership skills. Charles has redeemed himself in the eyes of the team and has demonstrated why he has achieved a senior management position within the company. During this final activity Charles has been stretched, but he has risen to the challenge. He can return home tired, but satisfied.

The next activity will give you an opportunity to think about how you can put motivation theory into practice with your team.

ACTIVITY 11

Consider the list of key motivators in the chart below. Beside each list up to three practical ways you can use this motivator to build a team climate where people work willingly and well.

Motivator	Practical things you can do to translate theory into practice
Physical needs *being comfortable*	1 2 3
Security needs *being safe*	1 2 3
Social needs *belonging*	1 2 3
Self-esteem needs *being appreciated*	1 2 3
Self-actualization needs *being challenged, having influence and ownership*	1 2 3

FEEDBACK

There are a number of ways in which you can turn theory into practice to motivate the people on your team.

MASLOW'S PHYSICAL NEED

Pay attention to the team's working environment and take appropriate and timely action to put things right when necessary. For instance, if someone complains that their office is draughty because of a broken window, or their chair causes back-pain, or the food in the canteen is diabolical, **don't** dismiss these complaints out of hand. Investigate the situation and try to solve the problem. Remember, if someone is cold because they're sitting in a draught, in pain because their chair is uncomfortable, or hungry because the food is inedible, satisfying their physical needs will be their **number one priority**. Your project, budget, report, schedule, presentation or whatever will come a very poor second on their list.

MASLOW'S SECURITY NEED
HERZBERG'S SECURITY MOTIVATOR

People need to feel a sense of security about the future and a measure of confidence regarding their continued employment. Although you can't promise job security if that is not likely to be the case, you can:

- let people know what you expect of them and how they are doing
- keep people informed about changes by being open and honest with information, and sharing this equally so that everyone knows where they stand
- be fair and impartial and treat everyone equally – no grudges, no favourites
- never, ever use the threat of loss of employment (through downsizing, for example) as a 'stick' to encourage people to work harder. This is a 'Theory X' manager's tactic, and it doesn't work. Instead of motivating people, fear acts as a demotivator and ultimately results in physical, mental and emotional stress.

MASLOW'S SOCIAL NEED
HERZBERG'S RECOGNITION MOTIVATOR

Because people need to feel accepted by society in general, and their friends, family and work colleagues in particular, you can make a real contribution to meeting this need by:

- creating a overall team atmosphere of approval. This involves **personally** avoiding gossip, back-biting and rumour-mongering, and demonstrating to your people that these activities have no place on your team

- celebrating individual and team success. Giving credit where credit is due. Acknowledging the long hard slog, as well as special efforts
- treating people as individuals and recognizing (and showing that you recognize) that everyone has a life outside of work
- including everyone 'in' – regardless of how you might personally feel about an individual
- providing resources and delegating tasks with fairness and objectivity

MASLOW'S SELF-ESTEEM NEED
HERZBERG'S INTEREST MOTIVATOR

People do best in jobs where they are challenged and stretched. Job satisfaction and the ability to feel good about their work are key motivators.

You can help by:

- allocating tasks to people which will use their skills to their utmost ability
- providing development opportunities so that people can expand their knowledge, skills and abilities
- making sure people have sufficient time and resources to produce high quality work
- carrying out regular performance reviews and appraisals
- providing constructive feedback
- listening to people, and taking them seriously
- noticing and acknowledging individual effort
- offering genuine encouragement and praise when it is appropriate
- appreciating that for some people status symbols and job titles are important for their sense of self-esteem and self-worth

MASLOW'S SELF-ACTUALIZATION NEED
HERZBERG'S ADVANCEMENT MOTIVATOR

- allow people the freedom to use their initiative and bring their own intellect and creativity to the job
- give people more responsibility than they expect (but keeping within the guidelines of what you know is possible and manageable for them)
- provide really challenging opportunities so that people can demonstrate their full capabilities and fulfil their true potential
- allow people to influence decisions
- enable people to take a real sense of ownership ('This is my idea, so I'm going to make it work')
- set up a 'self-fulfilling prophecy' by showing people that you believe in them, and that they are capable of achieving great things

Figure 8 below shows how people are likely to respond when the five basic needs are met, and are not met.

This is what happens when the need IS met	NEED	This is what happens when the need IS NOT met
■ complete ■ fulfilled ■ contented ■ sense of achievement	**Self-actualization** The need to do something which is challenging and stimulating and helps us to fulfil our potential	■ bitter ■ resentful ■ deep sense of lost opportunities and wasted chances
■ confident ■ valued ■ capable ■ sense of self-worth	**Self-esteem** The need to feel worthwhile and respected by others	■ angry ■ frustrated ■ worthless ■ low confidence ■ low self-esteem
■ normal ■ acceptable and ■ accepted ■ part of society/the family/the organization/the team	**Social** The need for companionship and to be an accepted member of a group	■ lonely ■ isolated ■ misunderstood ■ rejected ■ outcast
■ secure ■ safe ■ stable	**Security** The need to feel safe and secure and out of danger	■ frightened ■ anxious ■ physical ailments ■ clinical depression
■ ready to move on	**Physical** The need to eat, sleep, be warm, be comfortable, be pain-free	■ unable to concentrate on anything apart from pressing physical needs

Figure 8   What happens when the Five Basic Needs: (1) are met, (2) are not met

ACTIVITY 12

Consider each of the motivators listed below and rank them in importance **to you**. I is the most important, 7 is the least important. Please bear in mind that there are no 'right' or 'wrong' answers, and that no one motivator is more 'acceptable' or 'worthy' than another. (You may prefer to use a separate sheet of paper to preserve confidentiality.)

Motivator which encourages me to do something willingly and well	Order of importance
■ *Financial reward* (money: pay increase, bonus, pension top-up contribution etc.)	
■ *Status* and company 'perks' (important job title, larger office with better quality furniture, more expensive car, secretary or personal assistant, extended holidays etc.)	
■ *Security* (the security of knowing that your future is assured, that your job will last until you retire and then provide a reasonable pension, that you know – more or less – what the future holds)	
■ *Self-esteem* (being respected and valued for your contributions)	
■ *Recognition* (success; others having an awareness of your achievements; having a high profile; being known in your company or your community as a successful person; being recognized as someone of importance)	
■ *Self-fulfilment* (successfully meeting challenges; undertaking personally satisfying work; doing work which is of personal value and importance; making a 'real' contribution to society, or knowledge, or research; doing your 'own thing')	
■ *Acceptability* (knowing that what you do is approved of by others; being accepted by your peers; being recognized as an important member of the team; 'fitting in'; being liked)	

FEEDBACK

The motivator which you ranked as number 1 in the previous activity is the reward which is most likely to inspire you to work harder and faster. It is the factor which will encourage you to go the extra mile, and give it all you've got. The key point here is that **your** main motivator will, possibly, be different to the factor which motivates your manager, your secretary, the people on your team. By working out which reward will encourage your team members to give of their best will help you to build a high performance team.

Doug, Production Manager, motor industry

I used to think I was mainly motivated by money. Then I moved to a new job where I was paid considerably more than in the previous job. It took me about six months to work out that even though I was being paid a lot more I wasn't actually working any harder ... because I had been working as hard as I possibly could in the previous job. That's when I realized that the drive for security, rather than money, is my main motivating force.

Summary

- High motivation = High effort, and Low motivation = Low effort
- Professor Douglas McGregor's theory is that managers are either a 'Theory X manager' or a 'Theory Y manager':
    - Theory X managers believe that people are basically lazy, dishonest; they need to be controlled and disciplined and they can't be trusted to work on their own. To get the best out of people you have to keep on top of them and let them know what the consequences will be if they don't work hard and produce good results
    - Theory Y managers believe that people are basically honest and keen to work hard and achieve job satisfaction; that they enjoy challenging and interesting work. To get the best out of people you have to be prepared to delegate responsibility and allow people the freedom to use their initiative and creativity
- In the 1990s there are more Theory Y managers than there are Theory X managers. This is because Theory Y managers consistently achieve better results
- Frederick Herzberg devised the Motivation Hygiene Theory:
    - There are four motivators which contribute to people's satisfaction at work:
        - security
        - interest

- recognition
- advancement

■ There are a number of hygiene factors which cause people to be dissatisfied with their work. These include things like:
  - money
  - hours of work
  - holidays
  - pension rights
  - health care provision
  - parking, canteen and office facilities

■ Herzberg argues that people:
  ■ achieve job satisfaction through the motivators
  ■ suffer job dissatisfaction because of the hygiene factors

■ The hygiene factors are so-called because of the similarity between Herzberg's line of thinking and certain health care initiatives:
  ■ an efficient sewerage system does not make sick people well, but it does **help to prevent** cholera
  ■ a clean water system does not make sick people well, but it does **help to prevent typhoid**

■ Abraham Maslow created the Hierarchy of Five Basic Needs:
  ■ *physical needs* – being comfortable, warm, dry, pain-free
  ■ *security needs* – being safe and secure, out of physical danger
  ■ *social needs* – belonging to and being accepted by friends, family, work colleagues, society at large
  ■ *self-esteem needs* – being appreciated by others and having a strong sense of self-confidence and self-worth
  ■ *self-actualization needs* – being challenged and meeting the challenges, being able to influence and take responsibility for one's life and actions

■ Turning theory into practice means:
  ■ Physical need:
    - pay attention to the working environment
  ■ Security need and Security motivator:
    - let people know what you expect and how they are doing
    - keep people informed
    - treat everyone equally and fairly
    - don't use threats of job loss or major changes to try to improve performance
  ■ Social need and Recognition motivator:
    - create a team atmosphere of approval
    - celebrate individual and team success
    - treat people as individuals

- include everyone in team activities, especially social events – even if it's only a coffee in the canteen
- allocate tasks and resources with fairness and objectivity
■ Self-esteem need and Interest motivator:
- allocate tasks which will stretch and challenge people and allow them to use all their skills and abilities
- provide development opportunities
- provide sufficient time and resources so that people can do their best work
- carry out regular performance reviews
- provide constructive feedback
- listen to people and take them seriously
- notice and acknowledge individual effort
- offer encouragement and praise when appropriate
- recognize that status symbols and job titles have importance for some people
■ Self-actualization need and Advancement motivator:
- allow people to use their initiative
- give people more responsibility and more challenging work than they might expect
- allow people to influence decisions
- enable people to take ownership of ideas and projects
- help people to succeed by showing them that you believe they have the talent and the potential for success

Section 4 Performance management

Introduction

Performance management is the process of:

- setting objectives
- evaluating performance against those objectives
- providing feedback on performance

Performance management is an important aspect of team building, and needs to be undertaken whether or not your organization operates a formal appraisal system.

In this section of the Workbook we'll be looking at how you can use regular reviews to manage your team's performance.

Performance management and team building

Performance management isn't just a flavour of the month activity. It is a meaningful process which, when properly undertaken, will provide enormous benefit for individual team members, the team as a whole and the team leader.

When a group of senior managers was asked about performance management, these are some of the comments they made:

June, senior manager in a local authority:

My team now realizes that performance management is a constructive process. It's not about blaming, or pointing out weaknesses or threatening people. Performance management provides people with a regular opportunity to sit down with me and discuss what they're supposed to be doing, to what standard, whether or not they are, in fact, achieving the standard. If they're not achieving, then it's up to me to find a way – through individual development or training – to help them become more effective. That, in turn, enables people to gain greater job satisfaction – so performance management helps me to maintain good team morale and high motivation.

Mark, Partner in a legal firm:

We have a large practice which is divided into specialist teams – there's a conveyancing team, a litigation team, a matrimonial team and so on. I manage the conveyancing team and I use performance management processes as a way of looking back on what has been achieved, and looking forward to what needs to be achieved.

Andrew, senior producer working in television:

Everyone needs to know what they're supposed to be doing, and how they're doing. I use performance management meetings as an opportunity to give feedback to the team, and receive feedback from the team – that's an important part of the process. It has to be two-way communication.

Performance management is used to:

- **look forward to identify and agree:**
    - objectives
    - standards
    - schedules
    - workplans (including methods of working)
    - priorities
    - resources

  so that each member of staff is very clear about what has to be achieved, by when, to what standard, using which resources

- **look back to identify and agree:**
    - which objectives have been achieved, and which have not been achieved
    - which standards have been met, and which have not been met
    - which schedules have been adhered to, and which have been delayed
    - which workplans (including methods of working) have been successful, and which have not
    - which priorities were correctly ranked and achieved, and which were not
    - which resources were actually used, and which additional resources (if any) would have been useful

  so that the member of staff is very clear about what has to be achieved, by when, to what standard, using which resources.

    This part of the process should answer the following questions (to which just about everyone needs to have the answers):

- Am I doing OK?
- Am I achieving my targets?
- Am I supposed to be doing anything differently?
- Am I fitting into the team, and do people feel that I am contributing my fair share?
- Does the boss like the way I do things?
- Does the boss realize how hard I'm working?

MANAGING TEAM PERFORMANCE

It is important to begin by making sure that you are clear about the team's:

- vision
- goals
- strategy

On page 7 of this Workbook you will find details of a team activity which will help you to generate and agree these three key elements with your team members.

Once you are clear about the team's vision, goal and strategy, the next stage is to work out how each individual team member can contribute to the desired end result. You can do this by agreeing, with each person, what his or her individual objectives ought to be.

MANAGING INDIVIDUAL PERFORMANCE

The single most important benefit of systematic, regular performance management is that it enables people to **discuss** and **agree** what everyone (individually and collectively), is trying to achieve.

A key aspect of the process is making sure that individuals are aware of their organization's:

- policies (e.g. equal opportunities)
- objectives (e.g. establish a presence in the US market by September 1999)
- core values (e.g. concern for the environment, care for people, ongoing staff development)

It is important that every effort should be made to align individual and team objectives with the organization's policies, objectives and core values. In other words, everyone in the business should be 'singing from the same song-sheet'.

Identifying objectives for key result areas

A good way to identify the objectives for each individual on the team is to begin by identifying the key result areas for each job on the team. An example of key result area identification is shown in Figure 9 below.

Name:	Stan Beechey
Job title:	Senior Field Sales Person

| Key result areas: |

```
                        ┌──────────────┐
                        │ Prospecting  │
                        │ for new      │
                        │ customers    │
            ┌──────────┐└──────────────┘┌──────────────┐
            │ Liaising  │                │ Selling to new│
            │ and       │                │ and existing  │
            │ maintaining│               │ customers     │
            │ links with │               └───────────────┘
            │ Service    │
┌──────────┐│ Engineers  │                          ┌──────────────┐
│Maintaining│└───────────┘                          │ Servicing new│
│customer   │                                       │ and existing │
│records and│                                       │ customers    │
│administration│                                    └──────────────┘
│systems     │┌──────────┐              ┌──────────────┐
└───────────┘│ Supervising│             │ Identifying new│
             │ team of three│           │ overseas      │
             │ junior staff │           │ markets       │
             └──────────────┘           └───────────────┘
```

Figure 9   Identification of key result areas

Once a job is broken down into different key result areas, it is then possible to start clarifying and setting precise objectives for each area. For example:

■   Key task area 1:   Prospecting for new customers
     Objective: Identify twenty new customer leads each week

1   What are **your** key result areas? Complete the chart below by identifying each key result area within your own job. (*Note:* depending on the scope and range of your job, (a) you may not be able to complete each box with a key result area or (b) you may need to add additional boxes to accommodate all of your key result areas.)

| Name: |
| Job Title: |
| Key result areas: |

2   For each key result area you have identified, note down your key objective.

Key result area:	Key objective:
Key result area:	Key objective:
Key result area:	Key objective:
Key result area:	Key objective:
Key result area:	Key objective:
Key result area:	Key objective:
Key result area:	Key objective:

Dividing your job into key result areas should have been reasonably straightforward and, ideally, you should have had little difficulty identifying your key objective within each area. If you have had any difficulty with this activity, then it might be a good idea to schedule a meeting with your manager to discuss any aspects of this objective setting process which need clarification.

Use the next activity as an opportunity to identify, for each member of your team, their key task areas and their key objective within each.

ACTIVITY 14   A13.2

1   Begin by taking photocopies of the Key result area chart and the Key objective chart which you will find below. You will need two copies of each chart for each member of your team. (e.g. if there are five people on your team you will need ten copies of the Key Result Area chart and 10 copies of the Key Objectives chart)

2   You should begin by completing one copy of each chart for each member of your team.

3   Also distribute one copy of the Key Result Areas chart and one copy of the Key Objectives chart to each member of your team. Ask each person to complete the charts and return them to you within a reasonable time-frame, say, 5 days.

4   On your own, compare the charts you have completed for each member of staff with the charts they have completed for themselves.
    Note:
    ■   areas of similarity and compatibility
    ■   areas of difference.

5   Arrange a one-to-one meeting with each member of your team to discuss the charts and agree individual objectives.

| Name: |
| Job title: |
| Key result areas: |

Key result area:	Key objective:
Key result area:	Key objective:
Key result area:	Key objective:
Key result area:	Key objective:
Key result area:	Key objective:
Key result area:	Key objective:
Key result area:	Key objective:

FEEDBACK

The main purpose of the one-to-one meetings between yourself and your team members is to:

■ agree each individual's Key Objectives. You may find it helpful to refer to Workbook 1
  The Influential Manager which deals, in detail, with setting SMART objectives.

■ agree a workplan which will enable each person to achieve those objectives

Agreeing workplans

A workplan is a straightforward statement of:

■ what needs to be done, and to what standard
■ by whom
■ the date when the work will be completed

A workplan may also sometimes include details of agreed development opportunities. If, say, a member of staff needs to attend a particular training event in order to acquire skills or knowledge which he or she needs to complete the tasks outlined in the plan.

Checking actual performance against objectives

Once SMART objectives have been set (specific, measurable, achievable, realistic, time-related), comparing performance with the objectives is a fairly straightforward process.

Either the objective **has** been achieved, or it **has not.** Either way, there is a great deal to be learned from the experience.

- **if the objective has been achieved**, then people can build on success by repeating similar actions and approaches again, in the future.
- **if the objective has not been achieved**, then people need to address the following questions:
    - What prevented me from achieving my objective?
    - What could I have done that I didn't do?
    - How could I have tackled the situation differently?
    - What will I do next time, if I find myself in a similar situation?

The next activity will give you an opportunity to think back to an occasion in your career when you failed to achieve an objective, and to consider what might have contributed to your lack of success.

ACTIVITY 15

1   Cast your mind back to a specific objective which you failed to achieve. This could have been anything from, for example, producing a report to a specific deadline, to achieving market penetration with a new product. Note down your objective in the space below.
    The objective which I failed to achieve was:

2   Now consider the factors which, in your opinion, specifically contributed to your failure to achieve the objective. Note these down in the space below.
    The factors which contributed to my failure to achieve my objective were:

3   Now imagine that the same objective faces you today. You approach this objective with the benefit of additional skills, knowledge, experience and, of course, hindsight. What would you do differently in order to achieve your objective?
    To achieve the objective today, I would:

4   At the time when I failed to achieve my objective:
     I received feedback on my performance yes ☐   **no** ☐

5   Finally, consider the key learning points of this experience.
     (a) As a result of receiving feedback on my performance, I learned:

or

     (b) As a result of NOT receiving feedback on my performance, I learned:

FEEDBACK

Providing constructive, appropriate and timely feedback is a powerful tool for managing performance. Colin, a Communications Director, explains how lack of appropriate feedback affected his performance.

I used to work for to a woman who refused to tell me how I was doing … until things went wrong. So in the beginning I would sail along, thinking everything was fine and then suddenly I would be summoned to her office and told, in no uncertain terms, that I was incompetent, incapable of following instructions and just hanging on to my job by the skin of my teeth. This ritual happened a number of times, and then I started to ask her, at regular intervals, 'How am I doing?', 'Is this what you want?' and so on. It didn't help the relationship at all - I think she was irritated by my questions, and I was made to feel even more incompetent because I was asking. Fortunately, I was able to move on to another company. There I worked for another woman who was superb about providing feedback. We were both clear about what had to be done and because of the regular reviews we had together, we both knew where we stood. I learned a lot from both experiences, and make sure, now, that everyone in my team gets regular reviews – formal and informal – so that we can keep on top of things.

From the manager's point of view, the process of checking performance against objectives provides the answers to questions like:

■   How effectively did this person work?
■   How well was the task completed?
■   Should I choose the same person for a similar task in the future – or should I choose someone else?

- Did I brief this person properly? If not, do I need to make adjustments to the way in which I brief this person in the future? Do I need to make adjustments to the way in which I brief everyone on the team?
- Does this person need development opportunities, and what should my role be in relation to providing these?
- Does this person need formal training/learning opportunities?
- What, in particular, do I need to do to ensure that this person's performance improves in the future?

Performance management meetings

You can organize both informal and formal meetings.

- *Informal meetings* can take place over a cup of coffee, or in the car, on the way to an appointment. They can be used as an opportunity to check out, in general, how someone is doing and to determine whether or not problems are (a) likely to occur or (b) already occurring. Informal meetings can often lead to a formal meeting: 'I'd really like to talk to you about this in more detail – how about 2 o'clock tomorrow?'
- *Formal meetings,* at regular pre-arranged dates (e.g. once a month, once a quarter) will give you and your people a real opportunity to review performance and, ideally, address minor issues before they develop into real problems.

The key to successful performance management is to adopt a constructive and structured approach:

- recognize achievements
- provide constructive feedback
- agree a **joint** problem solving strategy, where necessary
- agree future objectives
- set a date for the next performance review meeting

Recognize achievements

By recognizing achievements you will be reinforcing the behaviour you want people to repeat. For example, if someone says to you, 'By the way, that presentation was great! The overheads worked really well. I appreciate the time you took', then you will be likely to approach the next presentation you make in a similar way. You will repeat the actions which brought you praise and recognition – because you'll want to generate more praise and recognition.

By recognizing achievements you will make people feel **valued.**

People who feel valued are more likely to be motivated, and work willingly and well, than people who do not feel valued. Don't make the mistake of thinking that if you don't mention something people will assume that you're happy with it.

Everyone **needs** to hear that they are doing well. People who don't receive positive reinforcement will assume the worst and move into a downward spiral. The effects of not receiving positive reinforcement are shown in Figure 10 below.

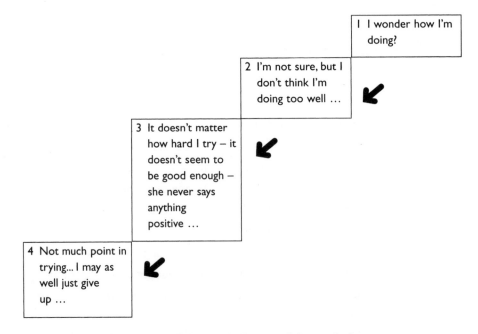

Figure 10 The effects of NOT receiving positive reinforcement

The 'Theory X' approach: 'Right – let's see what kind of a mess you've made of things' … is neither constructive nor helpful, and will not encourage co-operation, communication or productivity.

Constructive and destructive feedback

Constructive feedback is not necessarily the same as *approving* feedback. Constructive feedback draws our attention to areas of weakness in performance, but it encourages two-way communication and gives us the opportunity to think about positive improvements we could make. Constructive feedback helps us to see that, while there is room for improvement, there is also hope for the future.

Destructive feedback makes us feel angry and anxious. It relates not only to what we have done and how we have behaved, but it also refers to the kind of people we are and attacks our personalities, our views and our attitudes to life. Destructive feedback is demotivating, it makes us feel bad about ourselves and even worse about the person who is providing the feedback. It suggests that we are so useless, so incompetent, so worthless that no matter what we do, we'll never really get it right.

Constructive feedback:

- reassures
- encourages
- highlights those areas of performance or attitude which could be improved

ACTIVITY 16

Read through the case study which follows, noting down your answers to the questions which arise.

CASE STUDY

Rosa was asked by her team leader to prepare a budget for the new advertising campaign for a major client. Rosa spent four days and three evenings working out all the costings and making sure that the budget would be acceptable to everyone concerned. She persuaded the team's administration assistant to stay late to word-process the document, and Rosa herself, at some personal risk, used the electric binding machine to produce a beautifully bound document, for presentation to the client. Tired but satisfied, she left her work on her team leader's desk for inspection.

Rosa waited for three days for some feedback. She began to feel apprehensive. Was the budget OK? Had she covered everything? Should she have economized? Had she cut the costings too close to the bone? After four days Rosa really began to worry. It had been an important and responsible task, which she had tackled in the best way she knew how. Was she a disappointment? What should she do, she wondered.

At lunch time on the fourth day she saw her team leader in the corridor outside her office. There was no mention of the work she had done, no **feedback**. Rosa started to panic. Was her work so awful that her team leader was refusing to communicate with her? Gathering her courage, later that day she telephoned her team leader.

'What did you think of the budget I prepared?' she asked nervously. 'I haven't had time to read it yet', was the reply.

Question: At this point in the proceedings, how do you think Rosa is feeling?

Rosa left matters alone for a week and then decided she was going to find out whether or not her work was acceptable. She made it her business to visit her team leader in his office.

'Have you managed to look at the budget I prepared?' Rosa asked.
'Oh yes ... thank you,' came the reply.
'What did you think of it?' Rosa persisted.
'Parts of it were good ... but I'll have to re-work quite a bit of it. Some of the costings were way out ... Look I've got to dash, I'm supposed to be in a meeting now. Bye ...'

Question: If you were Rosa's manager, what improvements would you have made to this feedback and the way in which it was presented?

FEEDBACK

Constructive feedback should be:

- prompt
- specific about what has or has not been achieved and it should be delivered in order to:
- celebrate success
- suggest improvements which could be made

The next activity will give you an opportunity to evaluate your own feedback skills.

ACTIVITY 17 C13.4

Consider the following questions and then tick the appropriate box.

	Always	Sometimes	Rarely
1 Do you feel uncomfortable about giving positive feedback on performance?			
2 Do you feel uncomfortable about giving negative feedback on performance?			
3 Do you give feedback on performance by comparing one team member with another?			
4 Do you give feedback to people when you are tired, angry or otherwise upset?			
5 Do you check for understanding to make sure that the individual concerned is clear about your views and feelings?			
6 Do you feel more comfortable giving written rather than verbal feedback – e.g. sending a memo or e-mail?			
7 When giving feedback do you focus on specific behaviour?			
8 When giving feedback do you prefer to generalize rather than criticize specific points?			
9 When giving feedback do you prefer to talk more than you listen?			
10 When giving feedback do you ask numerous questions?			

FEEDBACK

Compare your answers with the score grid below. Add up the points in the boxes you ticked.

		Always	Sometimes	Rarely
1	Do you feel uncomfortable about giving positive feedback on performance?	10	5	1
2	Do you feel uncomfortable about giving negative feedback on performance?	10	5	1
3	Do you give feedback on performance by comparing one team member with another?	10	5	1
4	Do you give feedback to people when you are tired, angry or otherwise upset?	10	5	1
5	Do you check for understanding to make sure that the individual concerned is clear about your views and feelings?	1	5	10
6	Do you feel more comfortable giving written rather than verbal feedback – e.g. sending a memo or e-mail?	10	5	1
7	When giving feedback do you focus on specific behaviour?	1	5	10
8	When giving feedback do you prefer to generalize rather than criticize specific points?	10	5	1
9	When giving feedback do you prefer to talk more than you listen?	10	5	1
10	When giving feedback do you ask numerous questions?	1	5	10

The lower your score is, the better.

- score 10 – 14   Your feedback skills are excellent
- score 15 – 19   Your feedback skills are OK
- score 20 or over   Perhaps you should pay particular attention to the following points:

1 Positive feedback in the form of genuine praise and encouragement acts as a motivator to encourage people to give of their best.

2 Negative feedback enables people to see where and how they can improve. If they don't know they are not performing well, they can't and won't make changes.

3 Never compare one person with another, e.g. 'I don't know what your problem is Gillian … Simon doesn't seem to have difficulty meeting the deadlines.' This kind of feedback is neither useful nor helpful, and can lead to conflict on the team.

4 Never give feedback to someone when you are tired, angry or otherwise upset. If you are emotionally flustered you won't make a good job of it. Better to wait until you feel calmer, so that you can concentrate on what you want to say, and say it clearly and coolly.

5 Always check to make sure that there is genuine two-way communication and that the person who is receiving your message is clear about what you mean. Don't just assume they understand – ask. For example:
   – 'How do you feel about that?'
   – 'Tell me what you think about what I've said so far.'

6 Always try to give feedback verbally. A memo or e-mail can seem very terse, gives the other person no real opportunity for two-way communication (other than sending an equally terse written reply), and can lead to serious misunderstandings and bad feelings.

7 and 8 Always focus on specific behaviour which can be changed. Generalizations leave people guessing. Avoid general comments which target the whole person. Let people know precisely what the problem is and invite them to talk about it.

Don't say:

■   'You're becoming very careless'

Do say:

■   'We need to talk about the number of errors there have been in your work since the beginning of June. I understand that the last three sets of statistics you've produced all contained errors. What seems to be the problem?'

Don't say:

■   'You're upsetting clients'

Do say:

■   'I've had telephone calls from three different clients who, apparently, have been upset by you. What's been happening?'

Focus on specifics, e.g.:

'I need you to be in the office at 9 a.m.'
'I want you to wear a suit when we go to see D. Mitland'
'I'd like you to keep a written record of all your vehicle expenses'
You may find it helpful to refer to the section on assertiveness in Workbook 2, *Managing Yourself.*

9 Always listen more than you talk. Listening is a good way to find what the other person is thinking and feeling.

10 Always ask lots of questions to find out if the other person really understands the feedback – e.g.
   You: 'I think it's important that you keep a tighter rein on spending.'
   Tim: 'Right – OK'
   You: 'So where are you going to start making economies?'

or

   You: 'I think it's important that you keep a tighter rein on spending.'
   Tim: 'Right – OK'
   You: 'What is your initial target for cutbacks going to be?'

ACTIVITY 18

Assume, for the purpose of this activity, that you have arranged a performance review meeting with one of your team. You are not happy with this person's performance, and you need to work out the problem and agree a solution. There are four key stages which you and your team member, together, need to progress through during the course of the meeting. List these four steps:

1

2

3

4

FEEDBACK

STAGE 1 IDENTIFY THE PROBLEM

It isn't enough to say: 'Your attitude to clients is dreadful, and there's going to have to be an improvement'. Identify the problem clearly, so that there is no room for misunderstanding. For example: 'I've had telephone calls from three different clients who, apparently, have been upset by you. What's been happening?'

The other person might begin to bluster and bluff: 'Well, I can't think who that might be!'

Providing you have prepared for the meeting and have all the relevant information to hand, you can calmly present the facts: 'Jane Wright at Bryson Brothers said that on the 3rd March you slammed the phone down on her because she said she wasn't prepared to pay the extra delivery charge. Alistair McGregor at Lawtons on the …' and so on.

STAGE 2 ESTABLISH THE REASON FOR THE PROBLEM.

The reason behind poor performance could be anything from personal problems to lack of training and development opportunities; from inadequate resources to a personality clash with a colleague. The key thing here is to find out why a team member thinks he or she has not been performing well.

STAGE 3 DECIDE AND AGREE A PLAN OF ACTION TO SOLVE THE PROBLEM OR PREVENT IT FROM RECURRING

The plan of action will depend on the individual and the problem, but may include a number of options such as, for example, upgrading available resources, clarifying objectives or setting new ones, organizing development opportunities. It is important to ensure that the person involved agrees with and takes ownership of the plan of action. Rather than 'OK, I'll do this because you tell me to do it', there should be a real sense of 'Yes, I want to do this because I want to get it right'.

STAGE 4 MONITOR THE SITUATION

It isn't enough to have a chat, make a few suggestions and then walk away.
If you are serious about helping someone to improve their performance, you will not only agree what needs to be done, and give them the tools with which to do it, but you will also check to see how things are going.

If things are going well and there are measurable improvements, provide positive reinforcement. Praise and encouragement will motivate the individual to keep improving.

If things are not going well, let the person involved see that you are monitoring the situation and that while you are prepared to work with them to help them to improve, you're not prepared to take the easy option and let things slide.

Summary

- Performance management is the process of:
    - setting objectives
    - evaluating performance against those objectives
    - providing feedback on performance
- Performance management reviews are used to:
    - **look forward** to identify and agree objectives, standards, schedules, workplans, priorities, resources
    - **look back** to identify and agree which objectives and standards have been met, which schedules have been adhered to, which workplans have been successful, which priorities were correctly ranked and which resources were actually used
- A good way to identify the objectives for each individual team member is to begin by identifying the key result areas for that person's job, e.g.:
    - prospecting for customers
    - selling to customers
    - supervising team of three staff

- Once the key result areas are clarified, then key objectives can be set for each area. Key objectives should always be SMART – simple, measurable, achievable, realistic, time-related
- A workplan lays out details of:
  - what needs to be done, and to what standard
  - by whom
  - the date when the work will be completed
- Each individual on the team needs to know:
  - what the team is expected to achieve
  - what the individual is expected to achieve
  - time available
  - resources available
  - what to do if/when problems occur
  - how often the individual can expect feedback on performance
  - the criteria for success so that the individual will know when he or she have been successful
- When evaluating performance against objectives, you need to consider:
  - How effectively did this person work?
  - How well was the task completed?
  - If there is a similar task in the future, should I choose this person again, or should I choose someone else?
- When evaluating poor performance, you need to ask yourself:
  - Did I brief this person properly? If not, how should I brief this person in the future? Do I need to make changes to the way in which I brief everyone?
  - Would this person benefit from development opportunities?
  - Does this person need formal training?
  - What, in particular, do I need to do to ensure that this person's performance improves in the future?
- When dealing with people who are not achieving expected performance it is important to address, with the individual:
  - What prevented you from achieving your objective?
  - What could you have done that you didn't do?
  - Is there any way in which you could have tackled the situation differently?
  - If you find yourself in a similar situation in the future, how will you handle it?
- When conducting performance review meetings it is important to:
  - recognize achievements
  - provide constructive feedback
  - agree a joint problem-solving strategy, where necessary
  - agree future objectives
  - set a date for the next performance review meeting

- When offering constructive feedback:
    - enjoy giving praise and encouragement – they are proven motivators
    - don't avoid offering constructive criticism – if people don't know they need to improve, then they won't improve
    - never compare one person's performance with another person's performance. Playing good person/bad person will usually lead to conflict on the team
    - always check to make sure that people understand what you want them to do
    - feedback should always be given verbally. Memos and e-mail can lead to confusion and/or bad feeling
    - always focus on specific behaviour which can be changed and avoid generalizations or digs at someone's personality
    - always listen more than you talk. It's the only way to find out what you need to know
    - always ask lots of open questions and give the other person the opportunity to have their say
- Providing constructive feedback is a four-stage process:
    - identify the problem
    - establish the reason for the problem
    - decide and agree a plan of action to solve the problem
    - monitor the situation

Summary

Now that you have completed the thirteenth Workbook in this series, you should feel confident about your ability to:

- recognize the team role which each person on your team naturally prefers
- allocate work tasks in accordance with team role preferences
- use motivation theory to persuade your people to work willingly and well
- provide constructive and appropriate feedback to manage individual performance

In Workbook 13, *Building a High Performance Team,* we will be examining leadership styles, skills and strategies and looking at the ways in which you can consistently and skilfully empower and lead your high performance team.

Topics which have been touched upon in this Workbook are covered in greater depth in other books in this series:

- Workbook 1: *The Influential Manager*
- Workbook 2: *Managing Yourself*
- Workbook 9: *Project Management*
- Workbook 12: *Developing Yourself and Your Staff*
- Workbook 16: *Communication*

Recommended reading

Belbin, R. Meredith (1981) *Management Teams*, Butterworth-Heinemann

Belbin, R. Meredith (1996) *Team Roles at Work*, Butterworth-Heinemann

Jay, R. (1995) *Build a Great Team*, Institute of Management/Pitman Publishing

McCann, D. (1988) *How to Influence Others at Work* (2nd Edn), Butterworth-Heinemann

McGregor, D. (1974) *The Human Side of Enterprise*, McGraw-Hill

About the Institute of Management

The mission of the Institute of Management (IM) is to promote the development, exercise and recognition of professional management.

The IM is the leading professional organization for managers. Its efforts and resources are devoted to ensuring the continuing development and success of its members.

At the forefront of management standards, the IM provides a range of services for its members. These include flexible training programmes and a unique range of support services such as career counselling, enquiry and research facilities and preferential prices on IM publications and other IM products.

Further details about the Institute of Management may be obtained from:

Institute of Management
Management House
Cottingham Road
Corby
Northants
NN17 1TT

Telephone 01536 204222

We need your views

We really need your views in order to make the Institute of Management Open Learning Programme an even better learning tool for you. Please take time out to complete and return this questionnaire to Marketing Dept., Pergamon Flexible Learning, Linacre House, Jordan Hill, Oxford OX2 8DP.

Name:..

Address:...

....

Title of workbook:..

If applicable, please state which qualification you are studying for. If not, please describe what study you are undertaking, and with which organization or college:

....

Please grade the following out of 10 (10 being extremely good, 0 being extremely poor):

Content: ....   Suitability for ability level: ....

Readability: ....   Qualification coverage: ....

What did you particularly like about this workbook?

....

Are there any features you disliked about this workbook? Please identify them.

....

Are there any errors we have missed?
If so, please state page number: ....

How are you using the material? For example, as an open learning course, as a reference resource, as a training resource, etc.

....

How did you hear about the Institue of Management Open Learning Programme?:

Word of mouth: Through my tutor/trainer: Mailshot:

Other (please give details):...

Many thanks for your help in returning this form.

Institute of Management Open Learning Programme

This programme comprises seventeen workbooks, each on a core management topic with the latest management thinking, as well as a *User Guide* and a *Mentor Guide*.

Designed for self study through open learning, the workbooks cover all management experience from team building to budgeting, from the skills of self management to manage strategically for organizational success.

TITLE	ISBN	Price
The Influential Manager	0 7506 3662 9	£22.50
Managing Yourself	0 7506 3661 0	£22.50
Getting the Right People to Do the Right Job	0 7506 3660 2	£22.50
Understanding Business Process Management	0 7506 3659 9	£22.50
Customer Focus	0 7506 3663 7	£22.50
Getting TQM to Work	0 7506 3664 5	£22.50
Leading from the Front	0 7506 3665 3	£22.50
Improving Your Organization's Success	0 7506 3666 1	£22.50
Project Management	0 7506 3667 X	£22.50
Budgeting and Financial Control	0 7506 3668 8	£22.50
Effective Financial and Resource Management	0 7506 3669 6	£22.50
Developing Yourself and Your Staff	0 7506 3670 X	£22.50
Building a High Performance Team	0 7506 3671 8	£22.50
The New Model Leader	0 7506 3672 6	£22.50
Making Rational Decisions	0 7506 3673 4	£22.50
Communication	0 7506 3674 2	£22.50
Successful Information Management	0 7506 3675 0	£22.50
User Guide	0 7506 3676 9	£22.50
Mentor Guide	0 7506 3677 7	£22.50
Full set of workbooks plus *Mentor Guide* and *User Guide*	0 7506 3359 X	£370.00

To order: *(Please quote ISBNs when ordering)*

- College Orders: 01865 314333
- Account holders: 01865 314301
- Individual Purchases: 01865 314627

(Please have credit card details ready)

For further information or to request a full series brochure, please contact:

Tessa Gingell on 01865 314477